The Legitimacy of the Human

Other Works of Interest from St. Augustine's Press

Rémi Brague, *On the God of the Christians (& on one or two others)*

Rémi Brague, *Eccentric Culture: A Theory of Western Civilization*

Philippe Bénéton, *The Kingdom Suffereth Violence:*
The Machiavelli / Erasmus / More Correspondence

Albert Camus, *Christian Metaphysics and Neoplatonism*

Peter Augustine Lawler, *Allergic to Crazy:*
Quick Thoughts on Politics, Education, and Culture

Edward Feser, *The Last Superstition:*
A Refutation of the New Atheism

H.S. Gerdil, The Anti-Emile: *Reflections on the Theory and Practice*
of Education against the Principles of Rousseau

Gerhard Niemeyer, *The Loss and Recovery of Truth*

James V. Schall, *The Regensburg Lecture*

James V. Schall, *The Modern Age*

Pierre Manent, *Seeing Things Politically*

Marc D. Guerra, *Liberating Logos:*

Pope Benedict XVI's September Speeches

Peter Kreeft, *Summa Philosophica*

Ellis Sandoz, *Give Me Liberty:*
Studies on Constitutionalism and Philosophy

Roger Kimball, *The Fortunes of Permanence:*
Culture and Anarchy in an Age of Amnesia

George William Rutler, *Principalities and Powers:*
Spiritual Combat 1942–1943

Stanley Rosen, *Essays in Philosophy (2 vols., Ancient and Modern)*

Roger Scruton, *The Meaning of Conservatism*

René Girard, *The Theater of Envy: William Shakespeare*

The Legitimacy of the Human

Rémi Brague

Translation and Introduction by Paul Seaton

ST. AUGUSTINE'S PRESS
South Bend, Indiana

Manufactured in the United States of America.

1 2 3 4 5 6   23 22 21 20 19 18 17

Library of Congress Cataloging in Publication Data
Names: Brague, Rémi, 1947- author.
Title: The legitimacy of the human / Rémi Brague; translation and introduction by Paul Seaton.
Other titles: Propre de l'homme. English
Description: 1st [edition]. | South Bend, Indiana: St. Augustine's Press, 2016. | Includes index.
Identifiers: LCCN 2016012554 | ISBN 9781587314605 (clothbound: alk. paper)
Subjects: LCSH: Humanism.
Classification: LCC B105.H8 B7313 2016 | DDC 144—dc23
LC record available at http://lccn.loc.gov/2016012554

∞ The paper used in this publication meets the minimum requirements of the American National Standard for Information Sciences - Permanence of Paper for Printed Materials, ANSI Z39.48-1984.

St. Augustine's Press
www.staugustine.net

Table of Contents

Translator's Introduction   vii

Chapter I: Opening Movement:
The Rise and Fall of Humanism   1

Chapter II: The Threatened Human   23

Chapter III: The Illegitimacy of the Human?   39

Chapter IV: A Medieval Questioning of the
Legitimacy of Man: The "Sincere Brethren"   55

Chapter V: The Word "Antihumanism": Alexander Blok   72

Chapter VI: Contesting Humanism: Michael Foucault   89

Chapter VII: The Legitimacy of Modern Times?
The Case of Hans Blumenberg   112

Chapter VIII: Who Makes Man?   134

Chapter IX: Being as a Command   153

The Origin of the Texts   172

Index   174

Translator's Introduction

It is very difficult to keep up with Rémi Brague (1947–), even if you want to do so. You should want to do so because he is one of France's, and even Europe's, leading intellectuals: credentialed, laureled, and in wide demand. Depending upon your experience or image of "French intellectual," you may be surprised by him. For one thing, he is a Catholic, practicing and thoughtful. As such, he was the recipient of the Ratzinger Prize in 2012, named after another famous Catholic intellectual with a longstanding interest in Christianity, Europe, and modernity, Joseph Ratzinger, better known as the Pope emeritus, Benedict XVI.

In what is probably not a coincidence, both the Bavarian theologian and the French philosopher focus on "culture," making it central to their analyses of history, the present, and prescriptions for the future. The importance of the term and reality is visible in its cognates "cultivate" and "cult." Culture involves the human relationship to nature, self and other, and the divine. Both the German and the Frenchman observe and diagnose a cultural gigantomachia in Europe and elsewhere. For the Bavarian thinker the contest pits "secular culture" against "all the historical, all the religious, cultures." Secular culture was born in Europe and conceives man as possessed of reason and freedom, with the former's perfection found in scientific rationality and human freedom best articulated as a canon of rights. Faith is optional in human life, societally, it is a private matter, and it must not be found among the democratic city's authoritative elements. To cut to the chase: it is atheistic humanism purporting to be the vision of man and world required by democracy.

Against it, Benedict pits a different view of democracy and an ampler view of European culture, one rooted in its constitutive past but open to a future forged by those who have knit together the whole of Europe's experience. European culture was formed by Christianity, the religion of the creative Logos, and its fraught but fruitful engagement with the philosophical logos of antiquity.[1] Paul's apologetic efforts on the Areopagus were its first steps, the Hellenistically-informed *Epistle to the Hebrews* brought it into canonical Scripture,[2] and Justin, Philosopher and Martyr, gave it theological articulation.[3] Its culturally formative idea of man was as "the image of God" with a vocation to Truth and the Good, and the means and guides, natural and supernatural, to their attainment. True, the ideal was often belied by recalcitrant reality and

---

1 Benedict XVI, *The Regensburg Lecture* (St. Augustine's Press, 2007). "This inner rapprochement between Biblical faith and Greek philosophical inquiry was an event of decisive importance not only from the standpoint of the history of religions, but also from that of world history—it is an event which concerns us even today. Given this convergence, it is not surprising that Christianity, despite its origins and some significant developments in the East, finally took on its historically decisive character in Europe" (#29).

"We can also express this the other way around: this convergence, with the subsequent addition of the Roman heritage, created Europe and remains the foundation of what can rightly be called Europe" (#30).

2 James Thompson, *Hebrews* (Baker Academic, 2008). "[T]he book most rooted in scripture uses the vocabulary of Hellenistic philosophy more than any other NT document" (13).

"The author lives between the world of scripture and that of Greek philosophy. He is one among many early Jewish and Christian writers who struggled to describe their faith in the language of philosophy" (24–25).

3 Benedict XVI, *Church Fathers: From Clement of Rome to Augustine* (Ignatius Press, 2008). "Overall, the figure and work of Justin mark the ancient Church's forceful option for philosophy, for reason, rather than for the religion of the pagans . . . Philosophy . . . represented the privileged area of the encounter between paganism, Judaism, and Christianity . . . ." (19)

imperfect men, but the distinction between church and state, the inviolability of the person, and rights of conscience for both reason and faith, were and remain invaluable Christian contributions. Contemporary democracy need not fear theocracy from its erstwhile opponent, and its current malaise and manifold challenges should be a spur to reconsidering Christian faith's essential contributions to the moral foundations of democracy.

Well known within academic circles as an expert in classical and medieval thought, Brague came to the public's attention in 1992, that is, shortly after the collapse of Soviet communism, with a book entitled *Europe, la voie romaine*—Europe, the Roman way.[4] He was prompted to enter the public lists when the question of Europe again became urgent. On what bases should a Europe recently released from artificial divisions build its common life? Should they be simply democratic, simply modern, or should the full reality of European cultural history be taken into account? The answer to that pressing practical question necessarily involved posing the Socratic question, what is . . .?, to a post-Socratic object, Europe.

Brague's Catholic Socratic answer was learned, illuminating, and provocative, tinged with apprehension about contemporary Europeans' ability to live in keeping with Europe's distinctive nature, faithful to its constitutive vocation. Europe, he argued, was a distinctive cultural formation, compounded of the famous symbolic pair, Athens and Jerusalem, but brought together and mediated by Rome, the Rome of Regulus and Augustus, the Rome of Peter and Paul. World conquerors and world orderers, the Romans encountered the Greeks early on, and eventually came to recognize their subjects' superiority to them in forming and expressing our common humanity. Cato the Elder was the historical emblem of this recognition and reversal, while Horace immortalized it in his lapidary verse, *Graecia capta ferum victorem cepit*.[5]

---

4   Translated in English as *The Eccentric Culture: A Theory of Western Civilization* (St. Augustine's Press, 2009).
5   "Captive Greece captured the rude/wild/fierce victor."

As for the other Rome, the Rome conquered by Christian faith and blood, against Marcion (c. 85–c. 160) it held that the superiority of the new dispensation must not be purchased by its severing from the preceding revelation: the God of the New Testament is the God of the Old. Again, reality did not always correspond to ideal, but pagan Romans were schooled that their divinities must bow before a God long worshipped outside its borders, and followers of Christ such as Jerome learned Hebrew to understand the fullness of revelation. In Brague's striking formulations, the Old Testament is better called "the first" (*premier*), and it serves as Christianity's "permanent foundation."

In these complex ways, Europe's way was the Roman way, acknowledging its need for instruction in reason and faith, grateful for what came its way from without, not inclined to boast of its own intellectual and spiritual achievements except as faithful—albeit also creative—disciples. The latter element, creativity, was required not just because the two sources needed to be brought together, but because both were marked by an aspiration to "the universal."[6] Plato's Ideas and Yahweh-Elohim, Lord of Israel *and* of all humanity, oriented the Roman *mens et anima* toward the most encompassing Transcendence.

Nor, one might add, was the particular slighted. Socrates was never just a type of the philosopher, and biblical revelation focused insistently upon the individual or the particular—Abraham, Israel, Mary, the Incarnation itself. Christian theology in its turn made major contributions to the concept of the person, as it considered its confession of a Triune God, three Persons in one Godhead, and an Incarnate Word, the second Person become fully human.[7]

Against this complex attitude of receptivity and aspirational elevation, which flowered in the Middle Ages, Brague juxtaposed what he called contemporary "cultural Marcionism" and another

---

6   Gabriel Marcel nicely captured this paradoxical combination in his fine phrase, "creative fidelity."

7   Cf. Rémi Brague, *On the God of the Christians (and on one or two others)* (St. Augustine Press, 2013).

ancient temptation, Gnosticism. Contemporary Europe, he observed, increasingly sundered itself from any esteem or openness to the premodern past and its elevating models, and modern science, like the ancient heresy, presupposed that the world was indifferent to humanity, while adding that any viable order must be man-made. As I said, at the beginning of the 1990s Brague was more than a little apprehensive about Europe's future *as Europe*. This apprehension has deepened as the decades have passed.

To place the present work, *The Legitimacy of the Human*, within its wider context, a few words about two trilogies are required. (Keeping up with Brague is a full-time occupation.) The heavy lifting of the cultural analysis of European history was done in a series of works that dealt, successively, with defining themes in Antiquity, the Middle Ages, and Modernity. *The Wisdom of the World* (1999) brought to light the Greek articulation of the world as a *kosmos*; *The Law of God* (2005) deftly compared Jewish, Christian, and Muslim conceptions of divine law, that is, of the divine and its normative relationship with humanity; while *Le Règne de l'homme, Genèse et échec du projet moderne* (2015) articulated modernity's characteristic anthropology, a figure of being-human deemed sovereign over cosmos and Creator, defined and tasked with thoroughgoing "self-determination."[8/9] As the subtitle indicates, Brague argues that the deliberate project of thinkers like

8   *Le Règne de l'homme* is forthcoming from the University of Notre Dame Press. The title in English is *The Kingdom of Man: The genesis and failure of the modern project*. The opening phrase is from Francis Bacon, while "modern project" comes from Leo Strauss.

9   If these three hefty volumes were not enough, the same three periods were covered by yet another trilogy: *Introduction au monde grec. Études d'histoire de la philosophie* (Éditions de la Transparence, 2005), and *Au moyen du Moyen Âge. Philosophies médiévales en chrétienté, judaïsme et islam* (Éditions de la Transparence, 2006) added to our understanding of philosophy in its Greek origins and developments and its continuation and fates in the three religions. To them was recently added *Modérément Moderne* (Flammarion, 2014), which, as its title indicates, attempts to articulate a chastened, more "moderate," version of being-modern. It too is forcoming from St. Augustine's Press.

Bacon and Descartes and Hobbes to create a City of Man has failed; to quote Benjamin Constant, the nineteenth- century French liberal: "there are weights too heavy for the hand of man." Brague's criterion of success or failure, however, is rather distinctive—albeit absolutely basic, as befits a philosopher—and is argued with rare erudition and persistence. That criterion and that argument are the focus and burden of *The Legitimacy of the Human*.

At the end of *The Legitimacy of the Human*, Brague relates it (and another book) to *Le Règne de l'homme*: "This book of middle size, like the smaller *Les Ancres dans le ciel* which preceded it in 2011, is a sort of satellite of my voluminous *Le Règne de l'homme*."[10] Smaller in size than the chief planet, the satellite has two advantages over its gravitational superior: it contains "developments" that the larger work could only "summarize" and it speaks "more directly and with less precautions" than the "big book."

In keeping with the last feature, *Legitimacy* contains such direct affirmations as the following:

> [M]odern thought is short on arguments for justifying the very existence of men. This thought sought to build on its own soil, by excluding everything that transcended the human, nature or God. In so doing, it deprived itself of every Archimedian point. This exclusion renders it incapable of making a judgment on the very value of the human.

On the other hand,

> Now let us look at this "higher" which exclusive humanism denies . . . . This instance can be either God, or nature. In the two cases, the "higher" was considered and treated as something divine. To recognize an instance of this sort makes possible a legitimation of the human.

10 *Les Ancres dans le Ciel: L'Infrastructure Métaphysique* (Éditions du Seuil, 2011). Forthcoming as *The Achors in the Heavens*.

This is the alternative that Brague repeatedly puts before his reader and modern society as such. His argument on its behalf runs, briefly, as follows: Contemporary facts and possibilities—the possibility of nuclear annihilation, environmental degradation and worse, demographic decline to the point where nations' futures are in jeopardy—pose an existential question that Brague variously formulates for contemporary Western humanity: In the face of such threats to the very existence of humanity, can you affirm that it is good that humanity exists? Do you want the human adventure to continue? Can you provide credible reasons to do so?

The first passage cited above indicates that in Brague's judgment modern thought or philosophy cannot, and his erudition provides considerable evidence to support the conclusion. Then, having exposed the modern Emperor's inability to respond, Brague brings in a former King, the God of *Genesis*, creative by way of authoritative speech, who brings not just being but articulate beings into existence. His final creature, made in His own image and likeness, can hear His being-and-life-giving commands, reflect upon their logic and meaning, and, in turn, articulate for himself what the Creator authoritatively declared, that "it is very good" that the world and the human exist.

Brague thus attempts to bring old gods back into the new city.[11] In this way, too, he is a Catholic Socratic, albeit with a twist.

Paul Seaton
St. Mary's Seminary & University
June 29th, 2017
Feast of Sts. Peter and Paul

---

11 The phrase "to bring the old gods to a new city" was coined by Bertrand de Jouvenel. It inverts the charge brought against Socrates in Plato's *Apology*.

Chapter I
Opening Movement:
The Rise and Fall of Humanism

Here I would like to pose the question of humanism in its widest scope. It seems to me that it is this very framework that has undergone a radical change in the past several decades. Before this parting of the waters (and still today for some reactionary minds), "humanism" was a convenient way of designating what should be promoted, or at least defended, to wit: a certain value given to man and to what is specifically human.

I will begin by rapidly retracing four stages in the development of the humanistic idea. Then I will recall how these stages have been successively undone (I will pay special attention to the last of these stages). Then I will pose the question of the legitimacy of the human. And I will end with some thoughts on the resources that might allow us to find an answer.

The "third humanism" as a point of comparison

The situation prior to the one in which we live today allows itself, perhaps, to be rather quickly sketched by way of a comparison with the last attempt aimed at giving new life to the humanistic program, in other words, the project of a "third humanism." This expression was proposed by the philosopher Eduard Spranger in 1921, who used it in passing.[1] However, the most famous representative of the

---

1   E. Spranger, *Aufruf an die Philologie (An Stelle der Vorrede)*, in *Der gegenwärtige Stand der Geisteswissenschaften und die Schule* [1921], Leipzig, Teubner, 1925, p. 7.

movement it named was without doubt Werner Jaeger. The main idea of the German classicist was that classicism (which was identified with Hellenism) would be a still-living source capable of irrigating Western civilization, which would draw from it as from a fountain of youth. It was to provide points of reference that would be useful for putting the West back in order after the catastrophe of the Great War and the troubles that immediately followed. Jaeger considered his own enterprise, to use a Platonic image, as a "third wave," after the Italian Renaissance and the classicism of the Weimar Republic.[2]

At the remove of time, today one might smile at the naiveté of such an endeavor. However, it was not lacking in grandeur. As for myself, no one can expect me to attack the value of the teaching and learning of classical languages; quite the contrary.

Be that as it may, Jaeger supposed that classical formation could aid man in attaining a more adequate development of his own humanity. It was this human formation that for the longest time was considered to be the content of *humanitas*, which since Aulus Gellius had been recognized as the Latin translation of the Greek word *paideia*.[3] This is why the professors of classical languages and literature from the fifteenth century on were called *humanistae*.[4]

In this way, it was both understandable and right that the study and care of the heritage of Antiquity was called "humanism." It appears that this term first occurred in 1841, with the historian Karl Heinrich Wilhelm Hagen, who was close to the left Hegelian Arnold Ruge.[5] In 1859 the term entered the title of a book by the

---

2   Plato, *Republic*, V, 472a.

3   Aullus Gellius, *Noctes Atticae*, XIII, 17, M. Hertz ed., Leipzig, Teubner, 1877, t. II, pp. 84–85.

4   See A. Campana, "The Origin of the Word "Humanist"," *Journal of the Warburg and Courtauld Institutes*, v. 9 (1946), pp. 60–63.

5   K. H. W. Hagen, *Deutschlands literarische und religiöse Verhältnisse im Reformationszeitalter. Mit besonderer Rücksicht auf Willibald Pirkheimer,* Erlangen, Palm, 1841, pp. 58–60, cited in W. Stroh, "De origine vocum humanitatis et humanismi," *Gymnasium* n. 115 (2008), p. 564.

German historian Georg Voigt.[6] And the next year, a much more famous author, the Swiss Jacob Burckhardt, followed closely on his heels with his pioneering book on the civilization of the Italian Renaissance.[7]

All this rested on a presupposition: one must affirm man, or more exactly: the human. Since forever—and more than ever after two world wars and some particularly spectacular horrors—we are aware that really existing men are not always (in truth, are rarely) up to the heights of their own humanity. "The human" has always been a criterion more than an observation, belonging to the order of norms rather than description. But no one doubted the value of the human, which was something to promote, to advance. Even today the temptation is great, for every well-intentioned person, to plea for a fourth (or an nth-) humanism. And who today would not claim to defend this sort of humanism?

Our situation vis-à-vis the humanistic project

It is the first humanism, the one that founded and justified the "humanities," that seems to me to be currently threatened. The question of humanism has taken a new turn, one that is both more profound and radical. Previously it was asked: *how* can one promote humanism? This meant: how can one defend it against all the types of inhumanity? Today the question is rather: *should we* propose and promote a humanism?

Humanism itself is what some have it in for. Today one is almost entirely on the defensive, defending it against its critics. Schopenhauer's saying, with which he opened his essay on morality, is well known: "It is easy to preach morality, it is difficulty to

6   G. Voigt, *Die Wiederbelebung des classischen Altertums oder das erste Jahrhundert des Humanismus*, Berlin, De Gruyter, 1859.
7   J. Burckhardt, *Die Kultur der Renaissance in Italien. Ein Versuch*, in particular III, 4: "Der Humanismus im 14. Jahrhundert," in *Das Geschichtswerk*, Frankfurt, Zweitausendeins, s.d., t. I, pp. 476–80.

ground it."[8] One could adapt it as follows: "It is easy to preach humanism; it is difficult to establish it." And for myself, I would add: it is even easier to thunder against the enemies of humanism, whether the danger is real, exaggerated, or invented out of whole cloth.

May I be permitted to illustrate my point by a phrase borrowed from a book by the British philosopher and sociologist, John N. Gray. I do not have very much in common with this author, but he seems to me to have written something that sheds real, albeit stark, light on our situation. His sentence only indirectly concerns the humanistic idea, while bearing directly on the Enlightenment project (although the latter is not without some connection with the former). Gray writes: "In the period of late modernity in which we live, the Enlightenment project is affirmed above all out of fear of the consequences of its abandonment. . . . Our cultures are cultures of Enlightenment not by conviction, but by default."[9]

I therefore say in the same vein, as a thesis-statement (and in an admittedly lapidary formulation): what we understand today by "humanism" is not an affirmation, but the negation of a possible negation. *Our humanism at bottom is nothing more than an anti-antihumanism.*

The development of the humanistic idea

I now would like to show how we have arrived at this point by sketching the development of the humanistic idea. As I said earlier, the word "humanism" is of relatively recent vintage. As a matter of fact, the thing itself had to pass through a rather long period of incubation before coming to be crystalized in the term. However, it seems to me even older than that.

---

8   A. Schopenhauer, *Preisschrift über die Grundlage der Moral* [1840], in Werke, ed. W. von Lohneysen, Darmstadt, Wissenschaftliche Buchgessellschaft, 1962, t. III, p. 629.
9   J. N. Gray, "Enlightenment's Wake," in *Enlightenment's Wake. Politics and Culture at the Close of the Modern Age*, London and New York, Routledge, 1995, p. 144.

I will distinguish several stages that I will present in chronological order. I mark four. They communicate with one another, without, however, the previous one necessarily leading to the one that follows. On the contrary, the following stage results from a jump from the one that came before, and hence a choice that was not necessitated.

(1) Difference

In the first stage, man is understood as constituting a species that is substantively distinguished from others by certain properties he possesses exclusively. That man is something other than an animal however is far from going without saying. The man in the street, even today, is not always very conscious of his difference, and regularly projects sentiments, even intellectual capacities, onto his pets that are analogous to his ("my dog understands me, my cat speaks to me").

The distinguishing criteria were the subject of numerous stories that attempted to explain their appearance. These criteria, however, were not always positively evaluated. On the contrary, myths of so-called "primitive" peoples often attempt to explain why man is distinguished from the animals by explaining, for example, why he must work and that he knows he must die.

The initial decision perhaps left a trace in a change affecting the representation of the divine. In ancient Egypt, for example, the gods join a human body to an animal head, or vice versa. A Greek, Porphyry, interpreted this fact as testifying to an explicit concern to mix beasts and men (*homoiōs pou anemixan thēria kai anthrōpous*).[10] The gods of Greece, in contrast, are purely anthropomorphic.[11] But this fact suggests that the observation of a difference between man and

10 Porphyry, *De l'abstinence*, IV, 9, 2, ed. J. Bouffartigue, trans. M. Patillon and A.-PH. Segonds, Paris, Les Belles Lettres, 1995, t. III, p. 14.
11 See Hegel's reflections in the *Aesthetics* (*Ästhetik* [1832], ed. F. Bassenge, Frankfurt, Europaische Verlagsanstalt, 1955, pp. 420–22), and Feuerbach's in his *Preliminary theses for the reform of philosophy* (*Vorläufige Thesen zur Reform der Philosophie* [1842], # 22, in *Kleine Schriften*, ed. K. Lowith, Frankfurt, Suhrkamp, 1966, p. 129).

the animal easily leads to a claim of human superiority, which is a reason why the first of the stages that I have distinguished does not allow itself to be grasped clearly in its purity.

In any case, it was also in Greece that one finds the two classical definitions of the human, which bring into relief two important specific differences: one, *logos*—for simplicity's sake, let us translate it as "reason," although that is far from being adequate—thus defining man as "the rational animal"; the other, life in the *polis*, the city-state, defining him as "the political animal." Aristotle placed them in a comprehensive description of man which brought together each of the different aspects brought to light by his natural anthropology: man's upright posture, his orientation to look ahead and above, his hand with its fine sense of touch, speech, his face.[12]

Here, however, one finds a description of the human that omits any value-judgment. It can even slide from time to time into a negative evaluation of man. As of yet, it isn't clearly a question of his absolute superiority.

(2) Superiority

The second stage adds to difference, which did not yet include explicit valuation, a hierarchy in man's favor. He appears *better* than the other species. However, one doesn't go beyond the comparative to the superlative: he is not the *best* of beings.

Aristotle has a very nuanced view of the place of man. To be sure, man is "the best among the living beings" (*beltiston anthrōpos tōn allōn zōon*). However, he is not the highest thing in the world. "In truth there are many things that have a more divine nature than man" (*anthrōpou alla poly theiotera tēn physin*). For example, the elements "that compose the order of the world" (*ex hōn ho kosmos synestēken*)— Aristotle has in mind the celestial bodies—are clearly superior to him. And this superiority is even obvious (*phanerōtata ge*).[13]

---

12 See my work *Aristote et la question du monde. Essai sur le context cosmologique et anthropologique de l'ontologie* [1988], Paris, Cerf, 2009, chap. V, pp. 223–71.

13 Aristotle, *Nicomachean Ethics*, VI, 7, 1141a34–1141b1.

Six centuries later Plotinus takes up the same theme in his polemic against the Gnostics. They fear and disdain the cosmic powers, and grant man a greater value than theirs. That is why he recalls that "if men are something that has value vis-à-vis the other living beings, even less so do <the celestial spheres> exist to exercise tyranny in the cosmos, but rather to create order and beauty in it."[14]

In this second stage one can distinguish two ways of relativizing human superiority:

(2a) This superiority among natural beings pertains to the fact that among all the different productions of nature, man most fully realizes the intention of nature. She glorifies herself in him, it is not he who removes himself from the natural circle in order to construct a superstructure. Moreover, his status as the greatest success assures him greater proximity to the divine.

(2b) In the two biblical religions, the greatness of man is only relative, this time however not in a static manner, but dynamically. This grandeur is the result of a choice exercised by what in itself is the highest of all that exists, to wit: God. This choice does not depend upon man's merits: it is a free and gracious gift.

This is what the Psalmist says in a sentence that is the only place in the Bible, and one of the rare passages in ancient literature, where the question what is man? is posed: "What is man, that thou art mindful of him?" It is God who assigned to man that place that is his, and it is not the highest: "Thou has made him a little lower than the 'gods'" (*tehasserēhū me'at me-elohīm*), probably divine beings, perhaps angels (*Ps.* 8, 5–9).

Christianity bases the preeminence of man not on the properties of his nature, but on the Incarnation of the Divine Word in the man Jesus Christ.

These advantages confer a *dignity* on man. The idea is of Greek origin as much as biblical; it ran through the patristic and medieval periods before finding a thematic formulation in fifteenth-century

14 Plotinus, *Enneads*, II, 9 [33], 13, 18–20.

Italian, first of all in Gianozzo Manetti, who in 1453 inaugurated an entire tradition of treatises on the dignity of man.[15]

On the other hand, another tradition ran parallel to this optimistic vision, constituting its counterpoint: it was a tradition even older than the former, of treatises on the misery of the human condition, a genre that is at least as old as the tirade attributed by Socrates to the sophist Prodicus in a spurious Platonic dialogue, the *Axiochos* (366d–369a).

(3) Conquest

A third stage begins at the beginning of the seventeenth century. Man appeared as the being who ought to dominate the others, to apply his own measure to them, to constrain them, as needed, to bend to his ends. And the superiority of man is no longer granted to him by a superior being; it must be the result of man's own activity. It is no longer possessed at the start, peacefully or easily; it must be conquered with great effort. Man realizes his superiority by becoming the master of nature.

After the initial trumpet blast sounded by Bacon and Descartes, the idea ran through modern times and found its final flourish with Fichte. Finally, even Nietzsche, who considered man as "something that must be surpassed," left us an enigmatic sentence: "'Humanize' the world, i. e., make us feel more and more as masters therein."[16]

The continuity of the theme, however, should not mask a break in the tone that marks the entire project. In point of fact, one can distinguish two phases within this stage.

(3a) The first to have explicitly formulated this intention was the Englishman Francis Bacon, with his project of a "kingdom of

---

15 G. Manetti, *De dignitate et excellentia hominis*, ed. E. R. Leonard, Padua, Antenore, 1975.

16 F. Nietzsche, *Also Sprach Zarathustra*, Vorrede, 3, *Kritische Studienausgabe*, ed. G. Colli and M. Montinari, Berlin, De Gruyter, and Munich, DTV, 1980, t. IV, p. 14, and fragment 25 [312], "Spring 1884," t. XI, p. 92 = *Der Wille zur Macht*, # 614.

man" (*regnum hominis*).[17] A generation later, the Frenchman René Descartes ventured the phrase, man "as the master and possessor of nature."[18] But the formulation remained somewhat isolated with him. Bacon's, in contrast, was placed within a project of vast amplitude, which aimed at nothing less than the correction of the consequences of original sin, in other words, humanity's loss of mastery over the rest of creation. He sought the realization of the project in the application of the sciences of nature. With Bacon, it was still a matter of relieving human pain by augmenting the comfort of human existence.

(3b) With Fichte, no longer is it a possibility opened by progress in the sciences of nature; henceforth we are in the presence of a moral exigency, a duty. Nor is it any longer a question of any sort of conformity with nature: "I wish to be the lord of nature, and it ought to be my servant; I want to exercise an influence over it commensurate with my strength, but it must not have any over me." However, this was only a moral exigency on the part of the individual, an exigence that ran up against what appeared to be an absolute dependency of man vis-à-vis nature, the nature within him and without. It is realized by the work of men of flesh and blood. Thus, in a text of the same year: "For humanity this is not a simple pious wish, but an indispensable demand of its right and destiny, that it live on the Earth as easily, as freely, by giving nature imperious orders, as much of an authentic human life as nature allows. Man has the duty to work. [. . .] He must work without fear, with pleasure, with joy . . . ."[19] One should note that "to live in an authentically human way" is identified with "working." More than

17 F. Bacon, *Novum Organon. Aphorismi de interpretatione naturae et regno hominis*, Title and # 68, ed. W. Krohn, Darmstadt, Wissenschaftliche Buchgesellschaft, 1990, pp. 80 and 144.

18 R. Descartes, *Discours de la méthode*, VI, in *Oeuvres*, ed. Ch. Adam and P. Tannery, Paris, Leopold Cerf, 1902, t. VI, pp. 61–62.

19 J. G. Fichte, *Die Bestimmung des Menschen* [1800], I, in *Ausgewählte Werke*, Darmstadt, Wissenschaftliche Buchgesellschaft, 1962, t. III, pp. 288–89; then *Der geschlossene Handelsstaat* [1800], I, 3, *ibid.*, t. III, p. 452.

a generation before Marx, and more than a century before Ernst Jünger, man assumes the figure of the worker.

By the same token, it is the idea of dignity that is picked up again, better than the previous programs that only aimed at a comfortable existence, and which it was easy to reproach for a certain lack of nobility.

(4) Exclusion

The fourth stage is constituted by what one can call an "exclusive humanism." It established itself in the nineteenth century. According to it, man is the highest being, and he must tolerate no other one above him. The young Marx reinterpreted the myth of Prometheus in this way, employing a verse of Aeschylus which had Prometheus say: "In a word, I hate all the gods" (*haplō logō tous pantas ekhthairō theous*). In his doctoral dissertation, he wrote: "The credo of Prometheus [. . .] is [philosophy's] own credo, its own *non serviam* against all heavenly and earthly gods, who do not recognize human consciousness (*Selbstbewußtsein*) as the supreme divinity, before whom one must have no other divinity."[20] (I lightly altered the last phrase in order to highlight the (intentionally blasphemous) allusion to "you will have no other gods before me" of the Decalogue (*Exodus*, 20, 3).

As for Auguste Comte, a few years later he named humanity with a phrase that until then, and especially with Rousseau, designated God: the "Great-Being."[21] He even designated humanity with the name of "Supreme Being," which was applied to God from the seventeenth century on, and more than ever

---

20 K. Marx, *Differenz der demokitischen und epikureischen Natur-philosophie* [1841], preface, *Werke*, "Ergänzungsband," Berlin, Dietz, 1968, pp. 262–63; Aeschylus, *Prometheus Unbound*, v. 975.

21 A. Comte, *Discours sur l'ensemble du positivisme* [1848], "Conclusion générale," ed. A. Petit, Paris, GF-Flammarion, 2008, p. 452 ff. J.-J. Rousseau, third letter to Malesherbes, 26 January 1762; *Oeuvres complètes* I, ed. M. Raymond, Paris, Gallimard, "Bibliothèque de la Pléiade," 1959, p. 1141.

during the Revolution, when Robespierre attempted to establish its cult.[22]

This stage is interesting because it was to designate this strong version that the word "humanism" was coined, first of all in Germany, in August 1841, by Arnold Ruge.[23] It then passed into French, probably by means of Proudhon, who was in contact with Germany. It appeared at the same time in Victorian English, where the word *humanism*, alongside *secularism* (coined in 1846 by George Jacob Holyoake), then *agnosticism*, ventured by Thomas Huxley in 1869, served as a synonym for "atheism" to be used by the well-raised sort.

Today, what we have to deal with is this fourth and last stage. To be sure, we cannot consider a further stage because it has not yet manifested itself. On the other hand, it seems that such a new stage is highly unlikely because it is hard to imagine man being placed on a level even higher than God . . . .

Fusion of meanings

Such a conceptual use of the term was not without an influence on the historiographical employment of the term, which was simultaneous with the conceptual changes. Thus, Karl Hagen thought that humanism was indifferent to Christianity, even possessing an antichristian tendency. (In passing, let me say that that is completely without justification.) The same sensibility appears in Georg Voigt. In his work he attributes a key role to Petrarch. "To distill a good deal of meaning in a single word, the genius of *humanism* blew through the world conquered by him." One would expect the historian to then provide a definition of the loaded term that he just

---

22 A. Comte, *Système de politique positive ou Traité de sociologie instituant la religion de l'humanité*, t. II: *Statique sociale ou Traité abstrait de l'ordre humain*, Paris, 1852, chez the author *et alii*, chap. I, p. 61 & 63; chap. IV, p. 256.

23 See W. Rüegg, "Zur Vorgeschichte des marxistischen Humanismusbegriffs" [1950], *Anstöße. Aufsätze und Vorträge zur dialogischen Lebensform*, Frankfurt, Metzner, 1973, pp. 181–97, above all p. 186.

employed. However, with deliberate intent, he did not do so. We read just a little later, that Petrarch "brought the principle of humanism with its intellectual ferment into the modern world. But *instead of explaining what we mean, essentially, by "humanism," instead of analyzing the concept in its positive features, at the risk of not finding its core and only grasping its accidental features*, let us depict Petrarch in his struggle against what confronted humanism, as being contrary to it or its obstacle."[24] Voigt here senses the danger of intellectual confusion, which is to his credit. But what is less to his credit is that he then ignores it and makes of the logical requirement—which consists in furnishing the definition of a word one has introduced—a mere matter of taste: the phrase I underlined above was replaced in the second edition with a simple "I prefer [*lieber*] to depict Petrarch."[25] One would think one heard Melville's Bartleby . . .

Be that as it may, one can hardly make it clearer that the term "humanism" functions as a polemical weapon, serving less to define than to oppose. For the first time, and at the very birth of the term, it appeared, as I said above, that humanism at its core is not much more than an anti-antihumanism.

In Voigt's case, "the other," one must add, is "scholasticism." Later it is a question of "the contrast between humanism, i.e., the free power that wants to create everything from itself, and the faith of the Church, which approaches man like a monastic postulant."[26] The historiography of the Enlightenment, set in place ever since Bacon and developed by Voltaire, Gibbon and so many others, has here become something self-evident that one can simply assume.

The unraveling of humanism

Today it is the case that these three initial stages by which humanism gradually was brought to the point of incandescent excess have

---

24 G. Voigt, *Die Wiederbelebung des classischen Altertums oder das erste Jahrhundert des Humanismus, op. cit.*, p. 38.
25 *Ibid.*, Berlin, Reimer, 1880, pp. 70–71 (2nd ed. revised and corrected).
26 *Ibid.*, p. 49 (1st ed.); p. 84 (2nd ed.).

become the objects of a critique that seeks to destroy them. The fourth stage, exclusive humanism, has maintained itself, but at the price of some metamorphoses. We will look at them.

It is obvious that I just raced through the centuries with seven-league boots on. Now, however, I can be even more rapid because what it took centuries to construct has only taken a few decades to contest. The attack has been leveled against the three initial stages by and large in the reverse order of their appearance.

(3#) Far from seeking to be "as it were masters and possessors of nature," man does not have the right to subject the rest of living nature, much less to exploit it. Certain environmentalists speak that way. One can retrace this protestation against the project of the domination of nature by man to the American George Perkins Marsh and his *Man and Nature* (1864).[27] One also can find precursors in the movement for the defense of animals.

Still, one must distinguish. If, on one hand, certain voices defend a prudent, even parsimonious use of natural resources, there are other, more radical, ones that argue for a rapid human depopulation in the interest of humanity itself; and finally there are those who recall that man (abstracting from his concern for his own long-term survival) also ought to be "the guardian of his brothers," the other living species. Each of these, at the very least, seems to me respectable and worth discussing. But these perspectives easily slide into a second version.

(2#) Far from being the best of the sublunary beings, as the second stage claimed, man is worse than the parasites or the wild beasts because he represents a global threat to life. That man is an omnivore, and perhaps the only true one, is a fact found everywhere.[28] From Antiquity on, this fact was interpreted in a moral fashion as a sign of the universal rapacity of man, who would thus

---

27 G. P. Marsh, *Man and Nature or Physical Geography as Modified by Human Action*, ed. D. Lowenthal, Cambridge (MA), The Belknap Press of Harvard University Press, 1965.
28 See for example F. Bacon, *The Advancement of Learning*, II X, 2, ed. T. Case, London, Oxford University Press, 1969, p. 127.

be a "wolf down-everything" (*pamphagos*).[29] It takes on an urgent character however when, as in our time, human voracity risks causing all other forms of life to disappear.

Others therefore dream of a world freed from the presence of humans. This is the case of certain groups of what is called "deep ecology." To be sure, these are extreme cases. Thus we find the Internet site VHEMT (Voluntary Human Extinction Movement), which calls for a voluntary extinction of the human species.[30] It is interesting to note that this dream is much older than today. Here is the oldest version I have been able to find: "Trees will sprout, they will grow green, without any human hand to cut or even bruise them; flowers will grow in immaculate prairies, nature will be free without man to constrain it, and this race will be extinct, because it was cursed from its infancy."[31] These lines of the young Flaubert date from 1838, three years before the birth of the word "humanism" in its more radical sense.

More recent expressions of this hatred for the human, but which still antedate the ecological movement, are not lacking. In a novel by Alfred Döblin, for example. The context is a description, done in a deliberately excessive style, of the societies that will emerge in the coming centuries in Europe. In Berlin reigns the first of a series of "consuls." A character complains of the indulgence of the measures he takes: "He recommended castration. One should cut the testicles of male babies. Only then can one hope that in fifty years the Earth will have assumed its best appearance: wild plants in the prairies, perhaps two or three houses still inhabited by old humans, but the wild beasts already returning. The Earth thus untroubled, the perverse race of men finished. The entire Earth needs to be rid of man. [. . .] Man is a corrupt species. [. . .] The

29 See Plutarch, "Bruta animalia ratione uti," treatise 64, # 8, in *Moralia*, VI-1, ed. C. Hubert and H. Drexler, Leipzig, Teubner, 1959, pp. 89–90.

30 See www.vhemt.org. I owe my knowledge of this site to a book by Chantal Delsol.

31 G. Flaubert, *Mémoires d'un fou* [1838], chap. IX, in *Oeuvres complètes*, ed. B. Masson, Paris, Seuil, 1964, t. I, p. 234b.

"human" species is intrinsically unstable. It destroys, it devours itself."[32]

A few years before, the idea appeared among another novelist, the Englishman D. H. Lawrence. One of his characters, the painter Rupert Birkin, utters some pessimistic tirades that culminate in the following formulation: "If man was erased from the surface of the Earth, creation would continue in a marvelous way and begin a new chapter, this time without man. Man is one of the errors of creation, like the ichthyosaurs. If only he were to disappear, think of the magnificent things that would emerge from those now-freed days, things newly emerged from the creative fire [*things straight out of the fire*]."[33]

(1#) Far from distinguishing himself from the other natural species by a qualitative difference as the first stage assumed, man only differs by degree. One then can talk of "the end of human exceptionalism."[34]

Thus, people exercise their ingenuity in showing that his language or social organization are not essentially different from their animal prefigurations. They attempt to teach chimpanzees to speak. The functioning of human societies and the behavior of bonobos are compared.

Conveyed by the media, popularization exploits scientific results of this sort, some of which are undeniable; but it interprets them with a malign pleasure in order to humiliate man. Examples abound; I will only cite one: the observation that the ape and man have 95% of their DNA in common. From it, however, an ideological point is made: *therefore*, man is no more than an ape that was lucky.

In itself, this sort of reasoning is quite weak. One could retort that we ordinary mortals share 95% of the vocabulary of Proust

32 A. Döblin, *Berge, Meere und Giganten* [1924], III: "Marduk"; ed. G. Sander, Munich, DTV, 2006, p. 133.
33 D. H. Lawrence, *Women in Love* [1920], New York, Knopf, 1992, chap. XI, pp. 121–22.
34 See J.-M. Schaeffer, *La Fin de l'exception humaine*, Paris, Gallimard, 2007; and the response of P. Valadier, *L'Exception humaine*, Paris, Cerf, 2011.

or Celine. But the way these great writers combine these elements makes all the difference.[35]

In any case, what seems to me to be interesting in all this is not the scientific data, which I neither deny nor have the means of denying, but the sentiments to which they give rise and which therefore are symptomatic.

What exclusive humanism denies

I have covered the stages of the rise of the humanistic idea with seven-league boots, and even more succinctly showed how three of the steps that were climbed have been retraced. I kept the fourth stage for the end, and it is to it that I will devote a brief third part.

This last stage has not been contradicted, or only partially so. Exclusive humanism continues to exclude the figure of the divine, vis-à-vis which the two previous stages defined themselves. I obviously mean to speak of the God of the Bible, in his Jewish version as well as his Christian one, and before Him, of the "divine" (*theion*) understood in the style of Greek philosophy, of Plato, Aristotle, and the Stoics. After the destruction of this humanism, there is nothing higher than man.

Now let us look at this "higher" which exclusive humanism denies, and attempt to reestablish the way in which it was viewed by the vision of the world that preceded this exclusive version of humanism. This could be either God or nature. In the two cases, the "higher" was considered and treated as something divine. To recognize an instance or authority of this type made possible a legitimation of the human. But it also implied a limitation.

In paganism one can take the example of Aristotle. He recalls in passing, as something obvious, that politics does not manufacture man.[36] The city receives man from nature. Man is not his own product, nor of the interactive life he leads in the midst of the city: he is the product of nature. In this way man has an extra-human

35 See, already, Pascal, *Pensées*, Br. 22.
36 Aristotle, *Politics*, I, 10, 1258a21–23.

origin. To be sure, and Aristotle recalls it scores of times in different contexts, "man engenders man." But this would be impossible without the aid of the sun. The complete formula, which is only found once in Aristotle's corpus, is: "man engenders man, with the aid of the sun" (*anthrōpos [. . .] anthrōpon genna kai hēlios*).[37] Here "the sun" means, by metonymy, the entirety of the physical universe. Man constitutes the sublunary apex of this universe, in that all the properties of the living found dispersed among the other animals find in him the foyer where they come together.

In the other source of our culture, the Bible, man appears as the creature of a God who, this time, has personal qualities. Here the dominion of nature is not a *project* but a *task* (*Genesis*, 1, 28). To the extent that it is *proposed* to man, it maintains him within the status of a creature.

The return of the gods

I just said that exclusive humanism denies all species of the divine and, *a fortiori*, of gods. This, however, was to speak a bit precipitously.

It is true that the Greek sort of divine has been thoroughly deprived of its plausibility by modern science. We no longer can see Naiads in the streams, Dryades in the trees, Zeus behind the storm. At best we can do so as a literary exercise for aesthetes, or fantasy for children, as in the famous book by Kenneth Grahame, *The Wind in the Willows*, which succeeds in making the figure of Pan plausible for a few moments.[38] Nonetheless, as an adult, to seriously seek to experience a "pagan" divinity would presuppose willful blindness to our scientific knowledge and pretending to forget what we have learned about nature.

On the other hand, once the bolts of biblical religions have been sprung, other figures of the divine readily emerge. To speak of "the

---

37 Aristotle, *Physics*, II, 2, 194b13.
38 K. Grahame, *The Wind in the Willows* [1908], chap. VII: "The Piper at the Gates of Dawn."

return of the gods" has become a banality.[39] Nietzsche hailed this possibility in the name of Dionysos. And before him, and even more after him, we have seen even more disturbing divinities come forth, which do not necessarily present themselves as such, and which are quite diverse.

As I said earlier, Auguste Comte, who in his maturity had called humanity the "Great-Being" and the "Supreme Being," at the end of his life gave to the Earth the name of "great fetish," and he demanded for it a "just adoration."[40] To be sure, he did so in a work that even his most zealous disciples prefer to leave to the side. It still is the case that the phrase is very interesting. It is even revealing, because of its explicit echoes of the most primitive form of religiosity. Since then other divinities have resurfaced under the name of the Nation, Progress, History, Class or Race.

It is a perverse divinity that resurfaces, one that demands human sacrifices. Human sacrifices believed to have been buried since the angel of the Lord stayed Abraham's hand (*Genesis* 22: 12). The first to have identified the danger as being one of new idols, and having named one of these ("Progress") a "Moloch," was perhaps the Russian author Alexander Herzen, in a work written at the end of 1847 during his Roman exile.[41]

As different as they were, these new divinities had a common feature. It is contained in a phrase with which Camille Desmoulins

---

39 On this, one book: F.-W. Graf, *Die Wiederkehr der Götter. Religion in der modernen Kultur*, Munich, Beck, 2004.

40 A. Comte, *Synthèse subjective ou Système universel des conceptions propres à l'état normal de l'humanité*, "Introduction," Paris, the author and Dalmont, 1856, p. 14; see also pp. 23, 34, 50, 53–54, 107.

41 A. Herzen, C toro óepera, 1, in *Oeuvres en deux tomes*, Moscow, Mysl, 1986, t. II, p. 25; cited without reference in I. Berlin, *The Crooked Timber of Humanity. Chapters in the History of Ideas*, ed. H. Hardy, Princeton University Press, 1990, p. 16; see also E. Töller, *Masse = Mensch. Ein Stück aus der sozialen Revolution des 20. Jahrhunderts* [1919], cited in T. Schabert, *Modernität und Geschichte. Das Experiment der modernen Zivilisation*, Wurzburg, Konigshausen & Neumann, 1900, p. 82.

had ended the last article of the *Vieux Cordelier* before being guillotined, and which Anatole France made the title of a novel in 1912: "The gods are thirsty."[42] The expression is only found once in the body of the novel, where it expresses the novelist's own point of view.[43] That said, it was a character who is doubtlessly the spokesperson of the author who formulated it, in a prophecy (obviously formulated after the fact) announcing Napoleon. "Await a day when one of these bearers of the sword that you have divinized will devour you all like the monster of the fable devours the frogs. It is then that he will truly be divine. Because *gods are known by their appetite.*"[44] Two years after the novel the First World War began and showed that the Nation was in the first rank of these thirsty gods. In Anatole France's novel, the central character is a painter without talent who, become a judge on the revolutionary Tribunal, dispatched his fellows to the gallows in the name of Liberty, Equality, and Happiness. Later, another frustrated painter will kill millions of men in the name of Race, and a mediocre calligrapher will compare China to a sheet of paper upon which he was going to write a marvelous social poem, on the condition that he first would erase it . . . with the greatest of care . . .

In a *softer* way, well-intentioned authors define the sacred as "that for which one can die." I will remind them that it is no longer a question of the Sacred but the Holy. This is true since the Bible. Kant, in recalling that only a will can be holy, then Emmanuel Levinas, by highlighting that, literally, to be holy is not sorcery or witchcraft, both of which are connected with the sacred, have only refreshed our memory on this matter.[45] I would define holiness as

---

42 C. Desmoulins, *Le Vieux Cordelier*, VII, ed. M. Matton, Paris, Ebrard, 1834, p. 242.
43 A. France, *Les dieux ont soif*, ed. D. Leuwers, Paris, GF-Flammarion, 1989, chap. IX, p. 109.
44 *Ibid.*, chap. XIX, p. 212.
45 See E. Kant, *Kritik der praktischen Vernunft*, ed. K. Vorlander, Hamburg, Meiner, 1967, p. 140; E. Levinas, "Désacralisation et désensorcellement," in *Du sacré au saint. Cinq nouvelles lectures talmudiques*, Paris, Minuit, 1977, pp. 82–121.

the sacrality of the only thing that cannot, as such, be sacred: to wit, the will. And in the Holy I see not that for which one must, or can, die, but above all that which gives life.

We should point out that among the masks that these perverse gods wear, there is one to which a sect of "deep ecology" explicitly demands humanity be sacrificed. It very consciously gives it the name of a Greek divinity, Gaia, the Earth. It was the British chemist James Lovelock who proposed this term in the 1970s.[46] He did so in the context of a scientific hypothesis, itself worthy of discussion among competent judges, among whom I do not count myself. But since then the expression has been picked up by certain members of the New Age movement, this time with a mystical coloration.

The failure of atheistic humanism

In conclusion, this invites us to cast a glance at the philosophical decisions that have led to this situation. They are at the basis of modern practical philosophy ever since Hobbes.

This philosophy never runs dry when it comes to bringing forth rules for human living-together. And it is even very effective, in its very different styles. It succeeds in explaining in a very plausible way, that it is in the interest of men who form political society, i.e., the human race in its entirety, to renounce violence in favor of peace and mutual justice.

On the other hand, modern thought is short on arguments for justifying the existence of men. This thought has sought to build exclusively on its own soil, excluding everything that transcends the human, be it nature or God. In so doing, it deprives itself of every Archimedean point. This exclusion makes it incapable of making a judgment on the value of the human.

We therefore have to recognize a new fact that is not without importance. People attempt to disguise it with a thousand

---

46 See J. E. Lovelock and L. Margulis, "Atmospheric Homeostasis by and for the Biosphere—The Gaia Hypothesis," *Tellus*, v. 26, n. 1–2 (1974), pp. 2–10.

subterfuges. It seems to me to be more important to proclaim it from the rooftops. Not, to be sure, like a cry of triumph, but as the expression of a profoundly felt concern: *the atheistic project of Modern Times has failed.* Atheism is incapable of responding to the question of the legitimacy of man.

Father Henri de Lubac, S.J., spoke of the "drama of atheistic humanism" in a book bearing that title, which appeared at the end of the Second World War. This very lucid book profoundly examined the thought of Auguste Comte, Marx, Nietzsche, and ended with a chapter on Dostoyevsky as prophet. In his preface, de Lubac summarized the result he believed he had attained: "It is not true that man, as was sometimes said in the past, cannot organize the Earth without God. What is true is that without God he can only organize it against man."[47] de Lubac does not explicitly say against whom he opposes himself here, who denied the possibility of an atheistic civilization. But one could think of an entire apologetics of the nineteenth century, represented especially by Joseph de Maistre or in Spain by Juan Donoso Cortes.[48] Or his contemporary Charles Maurras, who made his own the criticisms that de Lubac addressed to Comte, whom he once considered his teacher. In any case, de Lubac maintained that atheistic humanism could very well found a civilization, but that it would be an inhuman civilization. In other words, that man could survive, but at the cost of the degradation of his humanity. In this way, atheistic humanism would sin against the adjective, not the noun: against the human, but not man.

I wonder, though, if de Lubac was not, despite everything, too optimistic. We need to risk a further step: exclusive humanism is

47 H. de Lubac, *Le Drame de l'humanisme athée*, Paris, Spes, 1944; a new edition is found in v. II of *Oeuvres complètes*, Paris, Cerf, 1998, p. 10.

48 J. de Maistre, *Considérations sur la France*, V, in *Écrits sur la Révolution*, ed. J.-L. Darcel, Paris, PUF, p. 133; J. Donoso Cortes, *Ensayo sobre el catolicismo, el liberalismo y el socialismo* [1851], I, 1, in *Obras completas*, ed. J. Juretschke, Madrid, Biblioteca de autores cristianos, 1946, t. II, p. 348.

quite simply impossible. Not because it would render man inhuman, but because it would destroy man in the most fundamental sense of the term. When left to its internal logic, it must destroy itself sooner or later. It is incapable of giving an answer to a fundamental question: precisely, that of the foundation. This is an even more urgent question today as man gives himself more and more means of taking his future in his own hands, of deciding freely what he will be, and perhaps even if he will be or not; and at the outside he might be able to give himself the means of deciding the fate of the entire universe.[49]

To take his life in his own hands was the dream of humanism, a dream that in itself was entirely praiseworthy. More and more it becomes a reality. Man has the means today of determining his destiny. This is why the question becomes pressing, to know if the decision to be taken will be made in favor of the continuation of the human adventure or its end.[50]

What do we need to do to cause the scales to tip towards a positive answer? Modern Times are able to produce numerous goods. And not only in the domain of material goods. We owe them several goods of a cultural nature, the legal state, for example, museums for all, music on cheap devices. However, there is one thing that Modern Times are incapable of saying: why it is good that there are men on the earth. We have goods in large quantity. That it is good that these goods have a beneficiary, this is what we cannot say.

Or perhaps we can. But to do so we must believe in Him who said on the sixth day of creation that, taken in its totality, it was "very good."

---

49 See D. Jou, *Reescribiendo el Génesis. De la Gloria de Dios al sabotaje del universo*, Barcelone, Destino, 2008, pp. 267–68.
50 See my work, *Les Ancres dans le ciel. L'infrastructure métaphysique*, Paris, Seuil, 2011, p. 62.

Chapter II
The Threatened Human

I prefer to formulate the central question of the present work as bearing upon "the human" rather than on "man." In doing so, I wish to profit from the double meaning of the adjective, which is sometimes merely descriptive, sometimes normative. In speaking of the humane treatment of animals, or the humanization of prison conditions, one is using it in the second sense. This usage is not without its bitter irony sometimes, with man being the only living thing that can be bestial. But this means that he must be recalled to his proper humanity, as an ideal towards which he must aim.

The Janus-faced adjective is helpful, because what seems to me to be in danger at the stage that civilization has now attained is itself dual. On one hand, threat hangs over the material existence of the human species on earth. But it also bears, and perhaps more essentially, on what makes man human, on the capacities for humanization found in man. It is clear that if the species "man" were to disappear from the surface of the globe, the question of how to preserve his humanity would no longer be posed. On the other hand, it could happen that a species *homo sapiens*, as "the featherless biped" (in Plato's phrase), would continue to exist, but despite, even because of, the loss of what makes it human properly speaking.

What threatens the existence of man as a living species is obvious, and here we only need to recall a few things. Weapons of mass destruction, whether atomic or chemical, the pollution of the environment, demographic extinction—in a few decades they have passed from nightmares to real possibilities. One only needs to listen to the daily media to hear them talked about, at least the first two. The third, which is perhaps even more serious precisely because it goes under the radar, hardly makes the headlines.

In contrast, the factors within man that sap and undermine his humanity, these are harder to grasp. That's why I propose to speak of them in greater detail.

The non-human as the measure of the human

One often hears deplored the disappearance of the type of education based upon ancient languages, typically called "the humanities." Ever since Cicero and Aulus Gellius, this learning traditionally received the name of *humaniora*. The study of good authors, "the classics," was thought to render the one who devoted him- or herself to them "more human" (*humanior*).

I myself am among those who have had the good fortune of benefiting from a tincture of classical studies during their secondary education; and by the same token I belong to those who deplore their decline.[1] However, in keeping with Spinoza's dictum, as a philosopher I must understand rather than bemoan, or at least try to do so. One must therefore connect the phenomenon with a much wider tendency, both in its amplitude and the time-frame it embraces. To do so, I would like to take the term "humanities" very seriously and draw out its implications.

A very real and objective fact causes, or at least favors, the disappearance of humanism in one meaning of the term, i.e., humanistic education, the "humanities." This phenomenon comes to view in a special way for those of us who are academics; but it can be seen throughout all of western culture. More and more, the humanities are losers to competition with the exact sciences. European, or Westernized, elites from the United States to Japan, and passing through India and China, receive a formation where the

---

1   See my "Perdre son latin?", preface in C. Suzzoni and H. Aupetit (editors), *Sans le latin ...*, Paris, Mille et Une Nuits, 2012, pp. 51–62.

emphasis is on mathematics and the natural sciences. These disciplines become the principal criteria for entering the leading professional ranks that have the highest level of responsibility—and remuneration.

Even the professions whose practice assumes the closest contact with human beings are performed by those selected and admitted to study because of their aptitude in mathematics, physics, and chemistry.

The case of medicine is particularly clear. Young people who from their earliest years dreamed of helping and caring for their neighbor find themselves excluded from medical school because they take too long to solve a problem in statistics. While, in contrast, those who were able to do math problems from their earliest days do not always have what it takes to deal with their patients with tact and empathy. In any case, it is not their studies that will give them these qualities. They have to obtain them from elsewhere, from the education they receive from their family, their social milieu, their religious communities. And in those who were not fortunate enough to receive these moral resources—who otherwise can be of an unquestionable technical competence—one observes a tendency to see their patients as machines that have broken down and need to be repaired. The emphasis today on the need for a holistic approach to the suffering person is entirely praiseworthy. The same is true with the introduction of courses in ethics in the curriculum. But I fear that they are only very inadequate remediation for the problem they seek to address.

Far be it from me to denigrate the sciences of nature. But they never deal with the human or, when they do, they do not deal with the human as such. Francis Bacon gave the knowledge of nature a new task, which was to be distinguished from simple contemplation and eventuate in action capable of relieving human suffering.[2] Since then we observe this paradox: we expect the improvement of the human condition, but by means of an increase in knowledge of the non-human.

2   F. Bacon, *The Advancement of Learning*, I, V, 11, op. cit., pp. 41–43.

Schizophrenia

However, this is only the symptom of something deeper, to wit: our civilization today exists in a state of schizophrenia. Let us begin by recalling that this is not the first time that Western man finds himself in this situation, and that he did not die from it . . . From Aristotle and Ptolemy until the scientific revolution connected with the names of Copernicus, Kepler, and Newton, we have experienced intellectual disjunctions between what rigorous science said was necessary and what experience pointed to as plausible.

Astronomy accounted for the heavenly phenomena by means of very subtle mathematical models. They certainly were very complicated, but effective in the sense that they allowed one to predict with a high degree of precision eclipses, conjunctions, and oppositions. But physics also showed that it was impossible that these models actually described the reality of things. They required eccentric spheres or epicycles whose actual existence was inconceivable. They violated the fundamental principles of Aristotelian cosmology, according to which every cosmic sphere had to have the Earth as its center. From this point of view—to take up a rapprochement proposed by Pierre Duhem—positivism, which voluntarily renounces the search for causes and replaces it with the writing of laws, represents the modern and generalized form of the attitude that the Ancients were obliged to adopt.[3]

As for the current situation, we recall the two tables that the English physicist Arthur S. Eddington spoke about at the beginning of his Gifford Lectures given in 1927 on the nature of the physical universe. One is the table on which we write or eat; it presents a continuous and hard surface. The other, in contrast, is constituted by atoms which, ever since Ernest Rutherford (1911), we know are separated by distances comparable (on another scale) to those that separate the sun from the planets that revolve around it. The "true" table is the one whose existence atomic physics reveals. The world

---

3   P. Duhem, ΣΩZEIN TA ΦAINOMENA. *Essai sur la notion de théorie physique de Platon à Galilée* [1908], Paris, Vrin, 1982, pp. 23–24.

that the science of nature unveils thus passes for the "true" world. But it has nothing to do with the world of our daily experience. And "the process by which the external world of physics is transformed by human consciousness into a world familiar to us is outside the field of physics." Moreover, those who devote themselves to physics "do not even desire . . ., as we would say in common parlance, 'to explain' the electron."[4]

In the wake of Eddington, Bertrand Russell expressed a similar idea by providing an ironic definition of matter, which we never perceive in its own nature, but always by means of objects that, at bottom, are fictions: it exists everywhere there is a probability for us to see phantoms.[5]

The science of nature in its modern version is thus a dehumanizing authority. It is, and knows that it is, dehumanizing, ever since its birth with the mathematical physics of Galileo. He had already fought against anthropomorphism, by making it clear that the colors that we perceive are purely subjective and are not true properties of things.[6] Following him, John Locke proposed the distinction that has become classic, between primary and secondary qualities.[7]

In our day, Michael Henry has recalled that modern man lives in two different worlds which do not communicate with each other. The scientist employs in his daily life a knowledge different from the one he produces in the laboratory. Hence, according to Henry, we face the threat of a new barbarism.[8]

---

4   A. Eddington, *The Nature of the Physical World* [1928], Cambridge University Press, 1953, Introduction, pp. XI–XIV, then XV.

5   B. Russell, *The Scientific Outlook* [1931], New York, Norton, 1962, chap. III, p. 74.

6   G. Galilei, *Diversi fragmenti attenenti al trattato delle cose che stanno su l'acqua* [circa 1610], in *Le Opere*, Florence, G. Barbèra, 1968 t. 4, p. 24; also see *Dialogo sopra i due massimi sistemi del mondo* [1633], I, ed. F. Flora, Turin, Mondadori, 2004, pp. 107–08.

7   J. Locke, *An Essay Concerning Human Understanding*, II, VIII, 9, ed. J. W. Yolton, London, Dent, 1965, pp. 104–05.

8   M. Henry, *La Barbarie*, Paris, Grasset, 1987, p. 23 ff.

The rejection of final cause and meaning

The modern sciences of nature, i.e., the mathematical sciences dating from Galileo, or those that take as their ideal this type of knowledge, are based upon a process of abstraction vis-à-vis all the dimensions of experience that are properly human. In the study of nature one finds no trace of human values.

Science refuses to answer the questions posed by man. The question of final cause, of "why?", is the one that allows us to understand actions. There is no need to specify that we are talking about *human* actions. That would be a tautology, because properly speaking, it is only man who acts. To understand is to understand why, for what end, with what intention, a human subject acts as he does.

One can therefore say, not without some irony, that the motto of modern science is fundamentally the same rule that governs the conduct of inferiors vis-à-vis their superiors in the army: "No need to understand!" The disciplined subordinate obeys orders because they are orders, and does not ask why they are given. In the same way, the physicist limits himself to writing in mathematical language the laws that govern the accompanying relations among phenomena. On the other hand, he does not ask—he is even forbidden from asking—why the laws are what they are. As needed, he seeks the complicitous aid of the philosopher, who will explain that the question is meaningless.

Consequently, even though they are immensely *valuable* because of their technical applications, and immensely *fascinating* because of the perspectives they offer to our curiosity, the sciences of nature are not *interesting* in the proper sense of the term.[9]

Modern science replaces the search for causes with the description of laws, as Auguste Comte and Claude Bernard (who followed

9   See "Is Physics Interesting? Some Late Ancient and Medieval Answers," *Graduate Faculty Philosophy Journal* 23:2 (2002), pp. 183–201.

Comte in this) understood and declared.[10] It began with the polemics of Francis Bacon against final causes, which he considered to be sterile and fruitless. Bacon himself was a mediocre scientist and he had no discovery to his credit; but he knew how to capture and convey the intellectual atmosphere that made modern science possible.

Therefore, everything depends on what one expects from final causes. If it is an increase of efficiency in the mastery of things, it is obvious that by definition they bring nothing of the sort. They are even an obstacle, since mastery seeks to bring in its own ends. If, in contrast, they serve to orient man in the universe, they are indispensable. Bacon himself noted that these final causes "obviously pertain more to the nature of man than to the nature of the universe" (*sunt plane ex natura hominis potius quam universi*).[11] For the Lord Chancellor, this meant they were questionable. However, one can also read the statement in a contrary way, as implicitly posing the question whether putting final cause in parentheses doesn't lead to the disappearance of the meaning that man needs to live.

And what if these irrepressible questions are precisely those that constitute the human? This would lead to the following paradox: modern science is at once the highest realization of man, the glory of the human spirit, and the most radical of the factors that lead to dehumanization.

Everything therefore leads us to believe that a certain anthropomorphism is necessary. It should not be suppressed but controlled, and above all given its just place. The contemporary German philosopher Robert Spaemann renewed the paradox by asking, where is reality given to us as such? It certainly isn't at the

---

10 A. Comte, *Discours sur l'esprit positif*, 1, in *Philosophie des sciences*, ed. J. Grange, Paris, Gallimard, 1996, p. 138; *Cours de philosophie positive*, 58th lesson, ed. J.-P. Enthoven, Paris, Hermann, t. II, pp. 719–20, 730, 736; 60th lesson, p. 771; *Discours sur l'ensemble du positivisme*, 1, op. cit., p. 78 and "Conclusion générale," p. 544; *Système de politique positive ou Traité de sociologie, instituant la religion de l'humanité*, Paris, Mathias, t. 1, 1851, pp. 66–68.

11 F. Bacon, *Novum Organon*, I, 48, *op. cit.* p. 110.

elementary level of the perception of material realities. In truth, our senses effect a very radical selection in function of our possibilities of action, which in their turn are oriented to the satisfaction of our needs. In contrast, persons are given to us—to us who are persons, as such.[12]

The interior abyss

What is even more astonishing, while at the same time even more disturbing—even more than the gulf that opens between man and nature revealed by science— is the chasm that opens in our knowledge of man himself.

Thus, for example, the man about which the so-called "neurosciences" speak has no correspondence with the experience we have of ourselves and other men. In a more or less vague way we all feel that the scientific description of brain phenomena passes by the real phenomenon, that is, what in us says "I" and addresses itself to a "you." An entire literature of popularization, whether produced by real scientists or by journalists who aim to mock the denizens of "fly-over country," works overtime to have us forget that uneasy feeling and make us believe that chemistry, computer science, or some other science, "explains" why we act.

However, "to explain" anything—this is what no science ever claimed to do, if one means by that "to make understandable." The neurosciences are not an exception, they too solely propose to describe the laws of the phenomena they observe, not to understand them. In point of fact, the nature of these phenomena only makes more obvious the extravagance of the claims of those who expect their scientific description to provide more intelligibility than they can.

Our knowledge of physiology has increased spectacularly during the centuries, and especially in the last few decades. However, one can legitimately ask if we have taken even a single step beyond

12 R. Spaemann, "Wirklichkeit als Anthropomorphismus," *Schritte über uns hinaus. Gesammelte Reden und Aufsätze*, Stuttgart, Klett-Cotta, 2011, t. II, pp. 188–215.

what Socrates affirmed in his prison: to describe the functioning of his bones and muscles (he knew nothing of the nerves) still doesn't explain his decision not to flee prison out of respect for the laws and customs that formed him.[13]

There's more. Another abyss yawns between facts and values. The world appears as axiologically neutral, as "value-free," in the sense in which this expression is itself axiologically neutral. Good and evil have nothing in the physical universe that corresponds to them. This view is the result of a long-term historical evolution, which I attempted to reconstruct elsewhere.[14] Our search for the good therefore appears as a way of going it alone, of introducing a rupture in the fabric of reality. And in this world we are not at home, but like strangers come from elsewhere, in the manner of the ancient gnostic myths.

Hence the constantly recurring temptation to found morality on what science, whether real or purported, teaches us about the movement of things. It can be a matter of the evolution of living species and the fundamental factors that govern them: struggle for life, natural selection, survival of the fittest. It can also be, on a lesser scale (but one that offers an easier handle for our action and hopes), the history of human societies, at least as one believes he has discovered their laws.

In the two cases, whether one is inspired directly by Darwin, or indirectly by the intermediary of his admirer and emulator Marx, that is, whether one adopts an evolutionary morality or a Leninist one, morality now consists in following the current, a running atop a flowing raft that carries us away willy-nilly. G. E. Moore subjected this type of morality to a devastating critique, with the example of his contemporary Herbert Spencer, who had attempted an ethics inspired by Darwin.[15] Nonetheless, attempts

---

13 Plato, *Phaedo*, 98b–99a.
14 *The Wisdom of the World: The Human Experience of the Universe in Western Thought* (University of Chicago Press, Chicago/London: 2003).
15 G. E. Moore, *Principia Ethica*, II, # 29–34, ed. T. Baldwin, Cambridge University Press, 1993 (2nd ed. revised), pp. 97–109.

in this vein never cease to appear one after another, although less from professional philosophers than from amateurs. They give witness to the pain of the rupture I spoke of above.

Technology: superfluous man

The scientific knowledge of nature is not restricted to the theoretical plane. It made modern technology possible. And technology has constructed a world in which man can barely find his place, intellectually and affectively. It is even possible that this world was designed to expel man in the most concrete way possible. The idea according to which machines are called upon to replace man, even to domesticate him, continues to haunt us.

Let's take a single example, doubtless the first in the list; it comes from Samuel Butler. He first of all presented the idea in an article entitled "Darwin among the machines." In this article written in 1863, thus four years after the publication of *The Origin of Species*, and therefore before the second great work of the zoologist on *The Ascent of Man* (1871), the English novelist developed an evolutionary vision of machines destined to supplant the humans who produced them. Butler sees in the perfecting of machines by man an equivalent of natural selection, and in the machines themselves "the sort of creature that will be the next successor of man in possessing supremacy over the earth."[16]

A little later, the novel which is doubtlessly his best book, *Erewhon* (1872), took up the theme again.[17] There is no mechanization in the society presented under the form of the literary genre

16 S. Butler, "Darwin Among the Machines," in *The Note-Books of Samuel Butler* [...], London, Fifield, 1912, pp. 42–47, preceded by an explanatory note, pp. 39–42; the text alone is reprinted in H. F. Jones and A. T. Bartholomew (ed.), *The Shrewsbury Edition of the Works of Samuel Butler*, v. 1: *A First Year in Canterbury Settlement and Other Early Essays*, London, J. Cape, and New York, Dutton, 1923, pp. 208–13; citation p. 210.

17 S. Butler, *Erewhon*, ed. D. MacCarthy, London, Dent (Everyman), 1962.

of voyages to imaginary countries. But the renunciation of machines is only one trait among many. This society is very much the opposite of ours (which is implicitly conveyed by the title, *Erewhon*, which reverses the word nowhere, one of the possible interpretations of Thomas More's coinage, utopia). The break with mechanization, formalized by forbidding any machine that goes back at least two hundred and seventy one years, belongs to the past. The reader becomes aware of this history when there is a mention of a museum where a few old machines are found.

One must await the last part of the novel to receive the explanation in the form of extracts from the book deemed to have unleashed the revolt against machines and a civil war which pitted their supporters and opponents. The adversaries having prevailed, every invention going back at least two hundred years was banished.[18]

The narrator conveys extracts from a "Book of machines" whose author attempted to show that the difference between machines and man is only one of degrees.[19] And not in favor of man, because machines calculate much faster than he can, and are never tired. The points on which machines are inferior to man only owe to their still rudimentary state. Their future evolution will allow them to surpass man, who then will become a sort of parasite on them.[20] Already, they "act on man and make him a man"—in the sense that it is technological progress that allowed the growth of the human population. The day will come, though, when man will be to machines what field animals are to man. However, we will be happier in this domesticated condition: "We have reasons to believe that machines will treat us gently, because their existence will depend in large part on us; they will govern us with an iron rod, but they will not eat us; they will need our services, not only in the reproduction and education of their little ones, but also to serve them as domestic servants, to gather food for them and to feed them, to return them to health when they are sick, and in order

---

18 *Ibid.*, chap. IX, p. 57; chap. XXII, p. 139; chap. XXV, pp. 162–63.
19 *Ibid.*, chap. XXV, p. 157.
20 *Ibid.*, chap. XXIV, p. 146.

to bury their dead or to transform their inoperative members into new mechanical forms."[21]

Since then, such representations have become well known. An American author, G. B. Dyson, used the title of Butler's article for a book. He explained that, after all, life is but a twisting path that allowed the mineral to attain to thought. Once artificial intelligence has attained its highest perfection, it will be able to dispense with the living kingdom. At most it will tolerate the latter, in particular man, who represents its summit, like the pets we keep around for our pleasure.[22]

To go further: the obsolescence of man?

From the point of view of technology, man appears as outdated, or at least as superfluous. The German philosopher Günther Anders also shows this in his provocative book, whose title I employ in the subtitle above.[23] In an earlier book, *Les Ancres dans le ciel*, I mentioned this fine work, but without doing more than a brief survey.[24] Here, I can take more time. And this time I find, not without some embarrassment, that several of the discoveries that I thought were original with me are already found in his book, perhaps less provocatively presented, but certainly there. I am therefore at once flattered that I had a predecessor of this caliber and disappointed to have to acknowledge that he preceded me on many a point.

It is true that Anders adopts a different perspective than I do, which is that of anticipation, while he analyzes the present state of our societies; he does so, however, by considering what happens in the most advanced of them, to wit: American society.

21 *Ibid.*, chap. XXV, p. 158–59.
22 G. B. Dyson, *Darwin Among the Machines. The Evolution of Global Intelligence*, New York, Perseus Books, 1998.
23 G. Anders, *Die Antiquiertheit des Menschen*, t. I: *Über die Seele im Zeitalter der zweiten industriellen Revolution*, Munich, Beck, 1956 et t. II: *Über die Zerstörung des Lebens im Zeitalter der dritten industriellen Revolution*, 1980 [here = Antiquiertheit, t. I and t. III].
24 See *Ancres dans le ciel* … , *op. cit.*, p. 79.

His point of departure is the rise in the power of technology since the industrial revolutions which have constantly succeeded one another and compete in trying to outdo one another. According to him, technology has taken control of man, whom it redefines in view of its own ends. The danger does not reside in a bad use of technology but, as with Heidegger, in "the essence of technology"[25] (bringing the two together makes for strange bed-fellows, because Anders constantly criticizes him). Technology humiliates man by producing artifacts that are more perfect than he is, ending in a kind of "dehumanization."[26] I will not follow Anders in all of his analyses, although I will underscore their great acuity and the art by which he brings to light the underlying reality, often by means of anecdotal examples. Here I will concentrate solely on the concrete dangers that threaten the survival of the human.

The worst of these, if one believes Anders, is the risk of a nuclear confrontation, to which, ever since Hiroshima, he returned throughout his life. That threat of the poisoning of the environment that supports life is never mentioned, if my memory serves me. And the danger of demographic extinction is only indirectly mentioned. The beginning of his oldest essay, a note in a personal journal that dates from 1942, however indicates that he had become ashamed to owe his existence to the blind and uncalculated process of being conceived and born; that's so old-fashioned. And a very interesting note indicates that the fact of being born is often the object of his denigration, even resistance, for the sake of the Fichtean ego or Heidegger's *Geworfenheit*.[27] Would the philosopher have been thinking of the concept of "natality" and the importance given to it by his wife, Hannah Arendt?[28]

25 G. Anders, "Die Antiquiertheit der Maschinen II" [1969], #4, *Antiquiertheit*, t. II, p. 126, see also p. 216.
26 G. Anders, "Über prometheische Scham," #6, Antiquiertheit, t. I, pp. 41–42.
27 *Ibid.*, *Antiquiertheit*, t. I, pp. 23–24, and note pp. 325–26.
28 On the history of their relations, see G. Anders, *Die Kirschenschlacht. Dialog mit Hannah Arendt*, Munich, Beck, 2011.

Faced with the real possibility ("feasible") of the annihilation of the human race, in his view nihilism took on the character of a not-very-serious moralizing declaiming.[29] If one excepts the small number who gave themselves over to despair during the previous century, there was almost no theoretician of morality who called into question the fundamental assumption that there will be and ought to be human beings.[30]

He, however, managed to dig to the foundations of the affirmation or negation of life, which meant that he had to confront the question of nihilism. This occurs when he takes up the classical question of Leibniz, reprised by Hermann Lotze (to whom Anders, strangely enough, seems to grant the paternity), in a reflection on the nature of nihilism: why is there something rather than nothing? The nihilist, who is "a disillusioned moralist," gives it a particular cast: "why does it matter [was eigentlich daran liegt], that something exists rather than nothing?"[31]

One can express the fundamental question of nihilism in another way, by asking: "why ought we to affirm the ought?" (Warum sollen wir sollen?) The state of necessity which nihilism represents does not allow itself to be refuted. At most one can understand it. In this case, one sees that ought-being is an isolated phenomenon (Binnen-Phänomen). The question of why duty is a duty cannot receive a reasoned response except from within a life to which one has already affirmed yes. In any event, it presupposes that life is in accord with itself, in agreement concerning the basis of arguments external to morality, even without basing itself on any argument whatsoever. In reading this, one thinks of Alyosha Karamazov, who said that one must love life, and only then the meaning of life.[32] Anders concludes:

29 G. Anders, "Die Antiquiertheit der Bosheit" [1966], #4, Antiquiertheit, t. II, p. 404.

30 G. Anders, "Über die Bombe und die Wurzeln unserer Apokalypse-Blindheit," #1, Antiquiertheit, t. I, p. 238.

31 Ibid., #20, Antiquiertheit, t. I, p. 300; see also "Methodologische Nachgedanken," #2, Antiquiertheit, t. II, p. 417.

32 F. Dostoyevsky, The Brothers Karamazov, I, V, 3, Moscow, ACT, 2006, p. 234.

"That it is morally desirable [*erforderlich*] that there is a world and man, behold what cannot receive a moral foundation."[33]

On the occasion of a critical examination of the concept of meaning, as we employ it in expressions like "the meaning of life," Anders demonstrates its emptiness. It is in this context that he writes:

> When we recognize that the ultimate meaning of a product to which we contribute is the annihilation of humanity, we then know what we have to do and what we have to abstain from doing. *The question* that goes further, for example, that of knowing *what meaning it can have that there is a humanity rather than none*, at most has meaning on the theoretical plane (even if it cannot receive any response), but *for "practical reason" it is without interest.*[34]

One can only agree, at least insofar as one takes the concept of practical reason in a non-technical sense (as the quotation marks indicate), as the way of regulating inter-human affairs.

For Anders, the question of meaning is vacuous and reveals an inability to escape metaphysics.[35] This declaration sounds strange when one recalls that it comes from a thinker who from 1945 on never ceased thinking of the possibility of the annihilation of humanity by means of atomic weapons. A few lines later Anders himself recalls this fact: since the end of the Second World War, "it is a question of the "*to be or not to be*" of humanity."[36]

Anders supposes that it goes without saying that we have the duty to reject the annihilation of humanity and everything that

---

33 I summarize, paraphrasing along the way, and citing partially, G. Anders, *loc. cit.*, II, V, *Antiquiertheit*, t. I, p. 323. See *Ancres dans le ciel* ... , op. cit., p. 130.

34 G. Anders, "Die Antiquiertheit des 'Sinnes'" [1972], VI, *Antiquiertheit*, t. II, p. 390.

35 G. Anders, "Sein ohne Zeit," #3, *Antiquiertheit*, t. I, p. 220.

36 G. Anders, "Die Antiquiertheit des 'Sinnes'," VI, *Antiquiertheit*, t. II, p. 390.

leads to it. But to what extent does man deserve to be saved? A few pages later, he makes use of the rhetoric on the insignificance of man in the universe that has been standard at least since Pascal: "We, the little worm that lives on the surface of a third-rate planet orbiting around a third-rate Sun . . . ."[37] Is it really worthwhile to assure the survival of such a despicable species of insect?

We find ourselves before a phenomenon that is strangely widespread today. On one hand, one does everything to humiliate man; on the other, man is elevated to the rank of something whose dignity is inviolable.

In the face of the danger of dehumanization, of even the pure and simple annihilation of humanity, "warmth is more important than meaning." It is not the metaphysician who should have the last word, but the philanthropist (*Menschenfreund*).[38] One thinks of the American philosopher Richard Rorty and the preference he gives to what he calls "democracy" over truth. It does remain to be seen whether a purely human warmth can overcome the limits that enclose the men who presently exist and help them become capable of also embracing those who are not born, whom I must decide whether to call into existence or not. In other words, it remains to be seen whether the philanthropist can last very much longer if he ceases to conceal a metaphysician.

37 G. Anders, *loc. cit.*, #13, p. 387.
38 G. Anders, "Sein ohne Zeit," #6, *Antiquiertheit*, t. I, p. 231.

Chapter III
The Illegitimacy of the Human?

We have seen that man or the human is threatened. Our spontaneous reaction would be to fly to his assistance. This is due in part to the elementary desire to save our own skin, because, after all, it's a question of us. It also derives from a chivalrous disposition which prompts us to go to the aid of whoever is attacked. Be that as it may, is it a healthy reaction?

It is here that the question that serves as my title comes into play, that of the legitimacy of the human. I will begin by distinguishing three neighboring questions, that of the charm or pleasant character of human life, that of human dignity, and that of the normality of man.

Legitimacy and charm

I earlier alluded to the difficulty of passing a judgment on man from the outside. To begin with: from what external position?

But more fundamentally, and to begin with, it is not certain that a judgment made from within the human condition would be favorable to it. If one turns to the ancient sources of our civilization, one sees that the Greeks cast a much more jaundiced look on life than a certain golden legend would have it, one that is still very much entrenched among our half-educated media types. This is the myth of a joyous paganism, "laid back," *cool*, which "Judeo-Christianity" would have poisoned. This is but one more lost paradise in a series that begins with the origins of history, in fact even before them: the idleness before the Neolithic revolution, the Egyptian harmony with their visible gods before the appearance of monotheism, not to mention the religiously harmonious Andalusia before the *Reconquista*, or the charming Aztec religion before the conquistadors.

This rosy legend was born with the German enlightenment, with Winckelmann and Lessing of *How the Ancients Represented Death*.[1] It was used in the classics of Weimar. And, finally, it has exercised its influence over minds of much lesser quality up to our day. All these thinkers presented the pagan world as an example of serene peacefulness, of the calm affirmation of the goodness of life and of sensual pleasure.

However, not much remains of this myth since the devastating critique effected by the 1835 doctoral dissertation of Ernst von Lasaulx. This Bavarian classicist was an engaging personality, the student and friend of Franz von Baader, the student, friend, then son-in-law of Joseph von Görres. In his thesis he clearly states the thinker he takes on: Goethe.[2] Among the numerous witnesses to the "pessimism" of the Greeks that he nearly exhaustively catalogues, I will cite only three. Herodotus recounts the story of Cleobis and Biton, two brothers whose mother had asked the gods, what was best for them? They died immediately in their sleep: the gods would thus have shown that "for man, to be dead is better than to be alive."[3] A chorus of the last tragedy of Sophocles sums up this way of looking at things in a phrase that I will translate in a deliberately loose way: "Not to be born beats all the records" (*m phunai ton hapanta nikā logon*).[4] Finally, the Latin poet Statius

1   G. E. Lessing, *Wie die Alten den Tod gebildet. Eine Untersuchung*, in *Werke*, Munich, Hanser, 1974, t. VI, pp. 405–62.

2   E. von Lasaulx, *De mortis dominatu in veteres. Commentatio theologico-philosophica*, Munich, Cotta, 1835, in particular p. 4, note 8; the work is reprinted in the collection of his works: *Studien des klassischen Altertums. Akademische Abhandlungen, mit einem Anhange politischen Inhalts*, Ratisbonne, Manz, 1854, pp. 459–94; p. 461, note 8.

3   Herodotus, I, 31, 3.

4   Sophocles, *Oedipus at Colonus*, v. 1225.

regrets that after the flood had cleansed it, the earth did not remain empty.[5]

If the Greek source of our culture reveals itself to be quite somber, its biblical source isn't rosier, and with it, the culture of the ancient Middle East in which it was rooted and from which it distinguished itself. In the Bible, Ecclesiastes "praises the dead more than the living, and more than all, those who are not yet born" (*Qoheleht*, 4, 2–3). (It is true that the author of this late text wasn't immune from Hellenistic influences.) Later, the Talmud reports a discussion between the schools of Shammai and Hillel on the question of whether God did well when he created man. At bottom the answer is negative. Nonetheless, now that the evil is done, it is important to draw the greatest amount of good possible from it by observing the Law.[6]

Since then, the oscillation between "optimists" and "pessimists," between smilers and grimacers, has not ceased. Treatises on the misery of the human condition follow one another, starting with the discourse attributed to Prodicus in the *Axiochos* of pseudo-Plato, until Lothar of Segni, the future Pope Innocent III, to which a host of treatises on the nobility of man would respond two centuries later in Italy.[7]

In any case, the question of the legitimacy of the human is not reducible to asking if life is worth living or not. Because, even supposing that human life is a constant series of pleasures, the issue would still not be joined. One would still have to ask if the

5   Statius, *Thebaid*, XI, 469–70, cited by C. S. Lewis, "Dante's Statius," *Studies on Medieval and Renaissance Literature*, Cambridge University Press, 1963, p. 96.

6   *Eruvin*, 136; see S. Pines and W. Z. Harvey, "Li-r'ot hak-kokhavim ve-ham-mazzalot," *Mehqarey Yer šalay m be-mahševeth Israel*, # 3 (1984), pp. 507–11; English translation in *Studies in the History of Jewish Thought* (*The Collected Works of Shlomo Pines*, t. V, Jerusalem, Magnes Press, 1996), pp. 89–93, esp. 93.

7   See above, n. #2, p. 18; Lotharii Cardinalis (Innocent III), *De miseria humanae conditionis*, ed. M. Maccarone, Lugano, Thesaurus Mundi, 1955.

happiness of man was not purchased at an excessive price for the rest of the planet.

Legitimacy and dignity

My question is therefore more radical: to know if the presence of man on this Earth, i.e., the mere existence of a being (a creature, if you wish) like man is legitimate. If this is not the case, every effort to defend something like the dignity of man would not only be bound to fail, but this failure would be a good thing.

Therefore, my question is not that of human dignity. That question is already quite complex if one treats it at the level of philosophical reflection.[8] This is even more true when, as is the case today, it is mixed with every sauce, and is used to justify every desire, including the most perverse. I neither have the need nor the desire to treat it.

Is the presence of man, or would his absence be, a good thing? And a good thing for whom or what? There has to be something that benefits from the existence or disappearance of the human species for it to be a good. Hence the claim of certain adherents of "deep ecology," who make the Earth that beneficiary, and bestow upon it a quasi-divine status, and even a special name borrowed from Greek mythology, Gaia. I have already pointed this out, and I will return to it.[9]

The question is posed with increased sharpness and urgency ever since the movement that calls for respect for the environment. Certain of its representatives, among whom the most extreme, give a negative answer. But it is no less heightened where a positive response is ventured. Indeed, one has to ask, supposing that the existence of man is a good thing, for whom or what would it be good? That it is a good for man himself, that is hardly surprising. To be judge and

8   See T. De Koninck, *De la dignité humaine*, Paris, PUF, 1995; W. Schweidler, *Über Menschenwürde. Der Ursprung der Person und die Kultur des Lebens*, Wiesbaden, VS, 2012.
9   See supra, p. 20 and below, pp. 139–140.

party in the case cannot be avoided. But we know that this situation can only produce biased judgments, which as such are quite suspect.

Less suspect, but even more injurious, are the negative responses. They however are found, and early on. Thus, the cynics of ancient Greece refused to grant man any value above the rest of the animals, even those that were commonly taken to be the basest. This is what one reads in one of the letters attributed to Diogenes of Sinope:

> One must neither marry nor have children. In truth, our species is weak. Now, marriage and children impose an additional burden of evils on human weakness. In every case, those who have married and raised children because of the assistance [they expect from them], but who have subsequently learned that these things bring with them many troubles, have come to regret them, when they could have avoided them from the outset. He who is without passions [*apathès*], because he supposes that his own [resources] suffice to live, will avoid marrying and having children. "But," you will say, "the world [*bios*] will become empty of humans. Whence will come the replacement [*diadokhè*]?" May it please Heaven that folly departs the world, once everyone will have become wise! In truth, the person who allows himself to be convinced by us will perhaps come to lack successors; but the rest of the world, who will not believe us, will have children. And supposing that the human race disappears, would that be something to lament any more than if the generation [*genesis*] of flies and wasps would come to an end? Arguments like that come from people who have not considered the nature of things.[10]

---

10 Pseudo-Diogenes, letter # 47, to Zeno, in *Die Kynikerbriefe, 2. Kritische Ausgabe mit deutscher Übersetzung von Eike Müseler*, Paderborn, Schöningh, 1994, pp. 74–76. The last sentence is cited by M.-O. Goulet-Caze in *L'Ascèse cynique* (Paris, Vrin, 2001, p. 56).

To be sure, this text is no doubt a forgery. It is one of those apocryphal letters, rhetorical exercises, that people loved to write and attribute to famous people between the second century before and the first century after Jesus Christ. To know whether it is worthwhile to marry and have children was one of the questions debated in Antiquity, where it received treatments that varied according to individual and school.

Moreover, one could allow oneself to venture the most extreme answers because the question only touched a small elite of philosophers and could not be extended to the masses, the "vulgar" (*hoi polloi*). Sociologically speaking, philosophers formed a very small circle, sometimes families, as we find among the last Neoplatonists, who were often related among themselves. The elitism of philosophers is constantly presupposed, and thus it was rarely explicitly acknowledged. Thus Porphyry declared in his treatise where he writes in favor of a vegetarian diet that it is not addressed to manual workers, but only to philosophers.[11] Here, as elsewhere, "the great limit of ancient civilization was its aristocratic character."[12] Our democratic societies, however, no longer can permit themselves to distinguish between what is good for the elite and what is good for the people.

The problematic of dignity has as its point of departure that men exist, and it asks how they should be treated with the maximum of respect. But it falls short when it is a question of justifying the very existence of men.

Legitimacy and normality

The question of legitimacy or non-legitimacy is not the same as that of the normality of man or its contrary, the strange character, the "eccentricity," of the human. The latter is static and comes from a

11 See, for example, Porphyry, *De l'abstinence*, I, 27–28, op. cit., pp. 61–63, et IV, 18, 7, *ibid.*, p. 31.
12 H.-I. Marrou, *Décadence romaine ou Antiquité tardive? IIIe-VIe siècles*, Paris, Seuil, 1977, p. 139.

synchronic description of the human which displays its distinctive traits and insists on their paradoxical character. Every anthropology even somewhat worthy of the name cannot fail to take into account that man possesses remarkable and exceptional features vis-à-vis the other living beings. This observation is in fact rather banal, the sole variety coming from the different traits upon which one places the accent.

Biologists have said that the human species is a deviation of nature. A philosopher like Max Scheler spoke (in French) of a "faux pas" and cited the idea according to which man would be the "ailing animal."[13] However, for Scheler this is a happy fault, and he draws an anthropology from the observation that is certainly tragic, but also quite optimistic.

On the cause of this "error" of nature opinions differ. Some, for example, point to the monstrous development of the cranium. This is mentioned by Max Horkheimer and Theodor W. Adorno, without indicating a source for the view.[14] In the same vein, the philosopher Helmuth Plessner puts at the center of his anthropology the idea that man is a "deserter from nature" (*Apostat der Natur*), which is to say that in the midst of its harmonious concert, he is a "trouble-maker" (*Unruhestifter*).[15]

The question of legitimacy as one of lineage

Moreover, the question of human dignity is static, while that of legitimacy is dynamic. Man possesses a dignity in virtue of what he is (his "nature"); in contrast, his legitimacy can only be founded on where he comes from (his "origin"). The question of legitimacy is therefore dynamic and diachronic; it implies a past history, a

13 M. Scheler, *Schriften zur Anthropologie*, ed. M. Arndt, Stuttgart, Reclam, 1994, pp. 46, 55, and 63.
14 M. Horkheimer and T. W. Adorno, *Dialektik der Aufklärung. Philosophische Fragmente* [1947], Frankfurt, Fischer, 1989, p. 234.
15 H. Plessner, "Der Mensch als Lebewesen," in *Mit anderen Augen. Aspekte einer philosophischen Anthropologie*, Stuttgart, Reclam, 1982, p. 29.

genealogy. In this, it connects with the most common meaning of the word "legitimacy," which distinguishes it from bastardy. In this way, language furnishes a precious indication. It is in this sense that Hans Blumenberg, about whom I will speak later, understands Modernity, as the quotation from André Gide shows which he puts as the epigram to the book where he argues in its favor. It is taken from *The Counterfeiters*, in a passage which explicitly concerns the nature of filiation: "It is curious how the perspective differs, depending upon whether one is the fruit of a crime or legitimate."[16]

The word "genealogy" has taken on a new coloration ever since Rousseau. Until then, genealogy was the ability to prove one's legitimacy by showing what was significantly called one's genealogical tree. More specifically, it attested a noble lineage. This was to prove one's right to certain privileges. With Rousseau, its aim was to bring to light an impure origin, it became an art of delegitimizing.[17] It was Nietzsche who produced the masterwork of this genre, the *Genealogy of Morals*. And Michel Foucault, and many others after him, took his place in this modern tradition of "suspicion."

The question of the legitimacy of man assumes a form that connects it with the contemporary sense as soon as one conceives that the human species descends from another species and, step by step, is the culmination of a lineage that goes back to the very origins of life. This way of seeing has imposed itself ever since Charles Darwin's *The Descent of Man* (1871) and, even if the details concerning the precise steps of the descent do not find agreement among scientists, the general idea is commonly held. To be sure, the popular slogan "Man descended from the apes" does not represent an exact description of the facts. It remains true that it conveys the humbleness of our origins.

16 A. Gide, *Les Faux-Monnayeurs*, I, 6, in *Romans, récits et soties*, ed. Y. Davet et J.-J. Thierry, Paris, Gallimard, "Bibliothèque de la Pléiade," 1958, p. 977.

17 J.-J. Rousseau, "Lettre a Christophe de Beaumont" [1763], in *Oeuvres complètes* IV, ed. B. Gagnebin and M. Raymond, Paris, Gallimard, "Bibliothèque de la Pléiade," 1969, p. 936.

In an opposite way, contesting human legitimacy can also consist in a verdict leveled against man, this time in view of the future. This is the case with Nietzsche. If man is something that "ought to be surpassed," and this is as much as a moral duty (*sollen*) as a physical necessity (*müssen*), it is because something or someone must take over for him.[18] That thing or that one will be greater than man in order to be up to the task that man can no longer bear.

In both directions, rearward or forward, legitimacy and its denial have a genealogical dimension: to have ancestors or to be oneself the ancestor of a lineage.

Three levels of legitimation

As for the question of legitimacy in the proper sense of the term, one can distinguish several levels where it can be posed. I have found three, which can overlap one another, at least partially. Legitimacy can concern:

(1) the action of man on nature, in particular his relations with other living species. As I have already indicated, this is far from having only positive consequences. The species *homo sapiens* is the most predatory of all. It does not limit itself to one prey. Man is omnivorous, and, if one can put it this way, he is even omni-utilizing, since for the satisfaction of his always-growing needs he requires the totality of what he can put his hands on.

The idea is not new. Towards the second century of our era, the authors of the writings known under the name of Hermes Trismegistus, the *Corpus hermeticum*, already echoed the question, was it truly reasonable to create man? Here was "an audacious

---

18 For *sollen*: Nietzsche, *Also Sprach Zarathustra*, "Prologue," 3, KSA, t. IV, p. 14; I, "Vom Krieg und Kriegsvolke," p. 60; for *müssen*: *ibid.*, I, "Von den Freunden- und Leidenschaften," p. 44; "Vom Freunde," p. 72; III, "Von alten und neuen Tafeln," 3, p. 248 and 4, p. 249; IV, "Der hässlichste Mensch," p. 332. Also see the question: "how to surpass man?" in IV, "Vom höheren Menschen," 3, p. 357.

enterprise" (*tolmèron ergon*). Man would explore the entire earth, dissect every living being, and leave nothing undisturbed.[19] In this reply, a question posed to Hermes, it is still Momos who is speaking, the personification of the spirit of critique and sarcasm. Since then we have adopted a more serious tone, but we hardly say anything different.

The Koran also poses the question when it reports the negative reaction of certain angels, including Iblis (= *diabolos*), before the divine decision to give them a successor (*khalîfa*) on the Earth (II, 30). I emphasize that it is a matter of giving a successor to the angels and not, as it is often said, a "representative" of God on earth. In any case, the objection of the angels is that man will shed blood.

It is not necessary to point out the contemporary relevance of this theme. Ecology recalls that the very existence of man is a danger for the other forms of life. That is especially true when he multiplies excessively, and even more so when he adopts an industrial way of life, one that is energy-costly and degrading. Granting that he would want to do so, would he be able to moderate himself? Does he do anything other than make the promises of a drunk or a politician? And finally, supposing that man does have an irrepressible tendency to go to the extremes, would not the surest remedy be to eliminate him?

(2) The presence of man on Earth. Several creation-myths of the origin of man explain that he isn't really in his proper place, but that he fell from elsewhere, whether it be spatially above, e.g., the celestial spheres, or somewhere better, like a garden of delights. I will return to some of these tales.[20]

Gnosticism considers man as the fruit of a fundamentally illegitimate birth, of a fall. Man is what ought not to have been. He was created by the Archontes "by premeditated design, in order to

19 Hermes Trismegistus, fragment XXIII (*Koré Kosmou*), # 44, in *Corpus hermeticum*, t. IV, ed. A.-D. Nock, trad. A.-J. Festugière, Paris, Les Belles Lettres, 1954, pp. 14–15.
20 See *infra*, pp. 143–144.

keep the spirit captive."[21] Gnosticism denies what some scientists of the past few decades have called the "anthropic principle": "Man was created *against* the world, man is superior to his creators."[22] In which case there still is illegitimacy, even if the tone is positive.

A character in one of Joseph Conrad's best novels, the German Stein, a planter and entomologist, for whom nature's greatest achievement is not man, but the butterfly, poses the question: doesn't man seek to occupy the entire planet precisely because he knows that he does not have a special place, that the world did not expect him, and does not know what to do with him?[23]

Among the works of Plato, the *Timaeus* gives the impression of a perfectly optimistic vision of the world. It concludes with a few lyrics of a hymn to the beauty of the world, which thus merits its name, *kosmos* (beautiful ordered whole). It appears to be the counterpoint of the *Phaedo*, to which "Platonism" is often reduced. However, looking closer at the text, the fullness of the world, which presupposes the presence in it of all the living species, is not completed except at the price of the fall of man. It alone allows the inferior beings, beginning—*horribile dictu*—with woman, all the way to larvae, passing through all the animal species, to emerge one after another from the original asexual male.[24]

(3) The very existence of man as a mixed being. This doesn't go without saying. Man realizes the union of contraries: an

21 H. Jonas, *La Religion gnostique. Le message du Dieu étranger et les débuts du christianisme*, trad. L. Evrard, Paris, Flammarion, 1978, p. 67; see also p. 267. English translation: *The Gnostic Religion. The Message of the Alien God and the Beginnings of Christianity* (Boston: Beacon Press, 1958).

22 I. P. Couliano, *Les Gnoses dualistes d'Occident. Histoire et mythes*, Paris, Plon, 1990, p. 19.

23 J. Conrad, *Lord Jim*, chap. XX, ed. C. Watts and R. Hampson, London, Penguin, 1986, p. 195.

24 The point was made by S. Benardete, "On Plato's Timaeus and Timaeus' Science Fiction," *Interpretation* n. 2, 1971, pp. 21–63, esp. pp. 41–42.

immaterial soul in a material body, where it is, as it were, enchained or "nailed." The question then is the legitimacy of being incarnated, of existence in the flesh. The task of legitimating the human consequently involves that of legitimating the flesh, of legitimating sensibility as having its own dignity, of defending it against the claims of pure intellect.

Neoplatonism asked why the intellect is present in a soul that is not purely intellectual, and why it is even lodged in a body at all? Plotinus asked what man is, in the sense of what constitutes man as such?[25] All of Neoplatonism, whether popular or learned, followed him in regarding the body with suspicion. It saw in the Christian idea of the resurrection a scandal, due to an excessive passion for the body (*philosomatia*): to want to recover one's body when death has discharged us of that burden, how perverse![26] It is amusing to recall this in our day when people love to reproach Christians for a (purported) disdain for the body, as Nietzsche's Zarathustra did in his critique of the "despisers of the body," repeated today by those not worthy to loosen the straps of his sandals.[27]

Closer to us, the Austrian engineer, philosopher, and novelist Hermann Broch wrote towards 1932 a short pamphlet in which he argued against the big deal that was made of man.[28] It has hardly attracted any attention. One has to acknowledge that it is not too clear. It seems however that his intention was to devalue the concrete individual for the sake of the moral subject, à la Kant.

---

25 Plotinus, *Enneads*, I, 1 [51].
26 See *ibid.*, III, 6 [26], 6, 71–74; Celsus in Origen, *Contre Celse*, VII, 36, ed. M. Borret, Paris, Cerf, 1969, p. 94.
27 Nietzsche, *Also sprach Zarathustra*, I, "Von den Verächtern des Leibes," in *Sämtliche Werke, Kritische Studienausgabe, op. cit.*, t. IV, pp. 39–41.
28 H. Broch, "Pamphlet gegen die Hochschätzung des Menschen" [around 1932], in *Philosophische Schriften* I [*Kritik*], *Kommentierte Werkausgabe*, ed. P. M. Lutzeler, t. X/1, Frankfurt, Suhrkamp, 1986 (2nd ed.), pp. 34–44.

End of the mediation

One can formulate the difficulty by employing an anthropological framework derived from Plato. The Greek philosopher defined man as a tripartite being: between the calculating faculty (*logistikon*) and the appetitive faculty (*épithumètikon*), mediation is assured by *thumos* (spiritedness).[29] The word originally meant breath, the audible respiration of whoever was tired out from strenuous effort. In the human body, the head where reason is seated and the abdomen where the desires are found are connected by the thorax, seat of the heart and lungs, which the diaphragm separates from the intestines. This is where Plato situated *thumos*. It is possible that Plato chose to assign to this dimension of the soul a mediating role because of one of the most singular features of respiration. It is the sole activity of the body that can be both instinctive and voluntary.[30] Be that as it may, it is the intermediary faculty, and not the two extremes of sensibility and the intellect, that make man, man. If we were only intellects, we would be angels; if we only had senses, we would be animals.

Now, according to C. S. Lewis, modern civilization displays a certain tendency to juxtapose the two extremes, the angelic and the bestial, without this mediating principle which alone makes us humans. We thus become, as he puts it in a witty but provocative way, "men without chests."[31] We perhaps are on our way to becoming what a thirteenth-century scholastic, the Franciscan Pierre de Jean Olieu (or Olivi), feared, when he evoked what men who were not essentially free could become: "beasts who are intelligent, or endowed with an intellect" (*bestiae intellectuales seu intellectum habentes*).[32] Or again: without mediation we are simultaneous man

---

29 Plato, *Republic*, IV, 439d–441b, and *Timaeus*, 69c–70b.

30 See my article, "Avoir du coeur: le sport et le 'thumos,'" in *Éthique, travail décent et sport*, École de Coëtquidam, Genève, BIT, 2008, pp. 57–59.

31 C. S. Lewis, *The Abolition of Man* [194], chap. 1: "Men Without Chests," New York, HarperOne, 2000, pp. 24–25.

32 P. de Jean Olieu (or Olivi), *Quaestiones in II Sententiarum*, q. LVII, ed. B. Jansen, Florence, Quaracchi, 1924, t. II, p. 338.

and beast, according to the image of the centaur that Machiavelli proposes to the prince who wishes to follow his counsel.[33]

The modern age is the moment when the vision of the world did without angels. For this vision, nothing blocks the view between the human and the divine. But nothing any longer assures their mediation. In our time, man perhaps compensates for this loss by the dream of himself occupying this place and being a pure sprit. Dostoyevsky let this been seen in an enigmatic passage at the end of Notes from the Underground: "It is even painful for us to be men, real men, made of flesh and blood; we're ashamed of that, we consider it to be shameful, and we would like to be a sort of universal men, who do not exist."[34]

On the other hand, one can observe an amusing reversal that owes to ecology: in the (neo-)platonic vision of the world, the troubling element was the body, with its sensible aspects which disturbed the circles of the intellect; but for some among us, it is rather the intellect that is thought to have disturbed the healthy naturality of the Earth. It is true that here it is a question of the intellect reduced to scientific and technological reason.

Extinction?

If one recognizes that the existence of man as a composite, as present on the Earth, or simply as dangerous for the Earth, lacks a foundation that can assure his legitimacy, and thus that man is something that ought not to be, the logical consequence is that man ought to disappear, that his extinction would be a good thing.

And one hears voices that preach the extinction of humanity by its own hand. Not necessarily in a violent way, as would be the case with a confrontation where weapons of mass destruction were

---

33 N. Machiavel, Il Principe, chap. XVIII, in Tutte le opere, ed. F. Flora and C. Cordie, Milan, Mondadori, 1968, t. I, p. 55.

34 F. Dostoyevsky, Carnets du sous-sol, II, 10, ed. M.-I. Brudny, Paris, Gallimard, "Folio bilingue," 1995, pp. 376–77 (the translation is modified).

used on a grand scale. Confronted with this danger, most men seek "to protect humanity against the dangers of this new engine of destruction." This is what Professor Calculus declares, who thus justifies his presence in a center for atomic research.[35] One rarely asks if it is good to act in this way, so much does it go without saying.

Now, the exceptions are always more interesting than the rule. A German philosopher and Anglicist, Ulrich Horstmann, intervened at the time of the debate over the installation of Pershing missiles in Western Europe at the beginning of the 1980s; and he did so in a very original way. The majority of the intellectuals among his compatriots pleaded either for maintaining the balance of forces to counterbalance the Soviet SS 20's, or for disarmament. But all chose as their ultimate criterion the maintenance of peace, and sought the most effective means to avoid a conflict. Horstmann to the contrary hailed the possibility, even the probability, of a nuclear war. He saw atomic weapons as the highly ingenious strategy which could permit the planet to do away with the one among the living things who represented the greatest danger to the planet, to wit: we ourselves.[36] And this was not a matter of satire or dark humor, the author having continued to defend the same position in his subsequent writings.

Moreover, it is not just for the other living things that the preservation of the human species would be an evil, but for each of the individuals who constitute it. In a play (its author says "a mystery"), Lord Byron puts on stage a dialogue between Lucifer and Cain. In it, the fallen angel unmasks sexual pleasure as "a pleasant degradation, a cheat that weakens and sullies us, a lure that encourages us to replenish the world with fresh bodies and souls, who are all predestined to be as weak and fragile as us, and as little likely to be happy." Cain responds that if this is so, he would prefer to die, "because to give life to those who can only

---

35 See Hergé, *Les Aventures de Tintin: Objectif Lune*, Tournai, Casterman, 1953, p. 9.

36 U. Horstmann, *Das Untier. Konturen einer Philosophie der Menschenflucht*, Vienna, Medusa, 1983.

suffer for so many years, then die, is nothing else, it seems to him, than to propagate death and multiply murders."[37] This passage is more precise than the kyrielle of texts that, since Buddha or Sophocles, affirm that it is bad to be born. This is the oldest text of the modern age that I have been able to find that reconnects with this theme, which is so frequent among the Gnostics. It curiously echoes what Schopenhauer wrote in his masterwork published three years earlier, but which remained ignored for several decades. The German philosopher, in contrast, knew Byron's works, and even cites *Cain* as "an immortal chef-d'oeuvre."[38]

Since then the idea has spread among the great herd of independent minds in the media, and even gained its titles of philosophical nobility. Thus, quite recently, a young South African philosopher named David Benatar (born in 1966) wrote a book published by a very respectable university press maintaining that procreating children is, from every point of view, a moral fault. If one takes the perspective of a morality of pleasure, not to exist certainly prevents one from experiencing a pleasure that is merely possible, but it totally avoids experiencing pain of any sort. Thus there is an asymmetry in favor of not-being. To produce beings susceptible to suffering is therefore reprehensible.[39]

How to respond?

37 Lord Byron, *Cain. A Mystery* [1821], act II, scene 1.
38 A. Schopenhauer, *Die Welt als Wille und Vorstellung*. II [1844], book 4, chap. XLVI, in *Werke*, ed. W. von Löhneysen, Darmstadt, Wissenschaftliche Buchgesellschaft, 1960, t. II, p. 570.
39 D. Benatar, *Better Never to Have Been. The Harm of Coming into Existence*, Oxford, Clarendon Press, 2006; see my *Les Ancres dans le ciel, op. cit.*, p. 92.

Chapter IV
A Medieval Questioning of the Legitimacy of Man: The "Sincere Brethren"

The dominion of man over the rest of living things has not always been thought to go without saying. Its modern calling-into-question is not a complete novelty. Here I would like to examine a few pre-modern examples, concentrating in particular on a medieval text.

Vegetarianism

Classical antiquity had already asked about the legitimacy of eating meat, and several philosophers declared themselves in favor of a vegetarian diet, basing themselves on the figure of Pythagoras, whether historically accurate or not. For him, to do without meat was to exalt man by having him adopt the diet of the gods.[1] The best known of these successors was Porphyry, who attempted to return to vegetarianism a fellow disciple and friend who had strayed from it, dedicating a treatise on abstinence to him.[2] The accent is placed less on the interest of the animals in not being killed and eaten than on the interest of man in not consuming a food that would compromise his well-being. Some foods taint those who eat them. One should abstain from those that excite the passionate part of our soul.[3] Moreover, meat is more difficult to obtain, prepare,

---

1   See M. Detienne, *Les Jardins d'Adonis*, Paris, Gallimard, 1972, pp. 78–113.
2   Porphyry, *De l'abstinence, op. cit.* [here = DA].
3   *Ibid.*, I, 33, 1, t. I, p. 67.

}55{

and digest. It therefore occupies too much of our time and renders the body more resistant to intellectual activity.[4]

The arguments that take account of animal victims rest on the idea of a closeness between men and the animals.[5] Or even that of a real kinship, based on the belief in the transmigration of souls, as was the case with Empedocles.[6] A good part of the second book of Porphyry's treatise is a critique of animal sacrifices, borrowed in large part from Theophrastus.[7] It also concentrates on the dangers that eating the flesh of victims pose to the one who eats it. Eating them could introduce foreign souls into them and disturb their access to the supreme God.[8]

It's not until the third book that Porphyry establishes that there are relations of justice between man and the animals. To do so, he must show that the animals also possess *logos*, understood as audible discourse and interior thought, and as intelligence.[9] In order to do so, he basically uses the stock of arguments accumulated by the Ancients and which one will see constantly recycled during the course of the intellectual history of the West.[10]

The "Sincere Brethren"

Now I would like to call to testify a passage from a medieval work. Its authors, still unknown, designated themselves under the name of *Ihwān as-Safā'*, "Sincere Brethren" or "the Brothers of Purity"— the second version having the advantage of reproducing the semitic

---

4 *Ibid.*, I, 46, 2, t. I, p. 79.
5 *Ibid.*, II, 22, 1, t. II, p. 89; III, 26, 1, t. II, p. 186.
6 Empedocles, DK 31 B 136 and 137.
7 Porphyry, *DA*, II, 5–32, t. II, pp. 74–99.
8 *Ibid.*, II, 48, t. II, p. 113. Jewish parallel in *Lettre d'Aristée à Philocrate*, # 147, ed. and trans. A. Pelletier, Paris, Cerf, 1962, p. 174.
9 Porphyry, *DA*, III, 2–18, 2, t. II, pp. 153–72.
10 See, for example, the arguments of Gryllos in Plutarch, *Moralia*, 64, "Bruta ratione uti"; and those of Alexander, in Philo of Alexander, *De animalibus*, ed. and English trans., A. Terian, Chico (CA), Scholars Press, 1981, # 17-76, pp. 73–100.

turn of phrase, which can replace the adjective with a substantive, while still retaining the idea of an elite of "the pure" which plays an important role in their thought, which is doubtless of Ismailite Shiite tendency. These writers composed about fifty treatises ("epistles") of unequal length, with the set forming a sort of encyclopedia. Their origin is probably Basra, the port in southern Iraq, and they belong to the second half of the tenth century.[11]

To my knowledge they are the first, other than some in the Far East, who posed the problem of the legitimacy of the dominion of man over the animals. The debate over this topic occupies the longest of their "epistles."[12] This text, the *Epistle of the animals,* has been called "an ecological fable," an anachronism intended to make it more popularly inviting, but which doesn't seem particularly apt to me.[13]

The remote sources of the tale are probably to be sought in India. Buddhism probably played some formative role in the origins of Islam.[14] And for obvious reasons of geographic proximity, the subjects of the Muslim empire had knowledge of the Indian religions. They were particularly aware of the challenge posed by

11 On them and their writings, the best works in French belong to Y. Marquet, among which: *La Philosophie des Ihwan as-Safā',* Alger, SNED, 1975.

12 I first cite *Rasā'il Ihwān as-Safā,* II, 8 [22], ed. B. al-Bustani, Beyrouth, Dâr Beyrouth, 1983, t. II, pp. 187–377, then *Epistles of the Brethren of Purity: The Case of the Animals versus Man Before the King of the Jinn,* English trans. and ed. L. E. Goodman and R. McGregor, Oxford University Press and Institute of Ismaili Studies, 2010 [here = *Animaux*]. There is a medieval Hebrew translation due to Kalonymos ben Kalonymos, *Iggereth Ba' aley Hayyin,* ed. I. Toporovski, Mosad ha-Rav Kook, Jerusalem, 1949 [here = IBH]. My friend Gad Freudenthal provided me a copy.

13 See L. E. Goodman, *The Case of the Animals Versus Man Before the King of the Jinn. A Tenth-Century Ecological Fable of the Pure Brethren of Basra,* Boston, Twayne Publishers, 1978.

14 See I. Goldziher, "Über den Einfluss des Buddhismus auf den Islam" [1903], trans. M. Gross, in M. Gross and K.-H. Ohlig (eds.), *Vom Koran zum Islam,* Berlin, Schiler, 2009, pp. 324–46.

a religion that did not recognize the idea of prophecy. That is why the barahima (brahmans) who argued for the superfluous character of prophecy are often found in Muslim apologetic treatises (*Kalām*).

In medieval Islam, the life of Buddha was known at least in its broad outlines, in particular the scene of his vocation after the encounter with the old man, the sick man, and the corpse. It figures in the *Barlaam and Josaphat*, which the Sincere Brethren knew.[15]

To have animals speak is also a regular practice in Indian literature. This is the case in the fables of Bidpai, the Panchatantra, which passed from India into Iran, then into the Arab world thanks to the adaptation of Ibn al-Muqaffa' under the title *Kalilah and Dimnah*, before it inspired occidental fabulists, with La Fontaine at the head.[16]

Islam also knew bloody animal sacrifices, which were established to commemorate the sacrifice, this time a human sacrifice, from which Abraham had been stayed by divine intervention. Buddha, in contrast, formally disrecommended animal sacrifices.[17] It therefore cannot be ruled out that the *Epistle of the animals* bears the mark of a Buddhist sensibility.

The plot

The scene is a marvelous island, rich in all goods and inhabited by all sorts of animals, until a group of men land there and reduce to slavery those who were not able to flee quickly enough. It is the men who reproach the animals for having fled, and who bring them up on charges. One will note that if the right of men to reduce

15 See *Épitres*, ed. al-Bustani, IV, 4 [45], t. IV, p. 58; parallel in IV, 7 [48], p. 175.
16 See Ibn al-Muqaffa', *Le Livre de Kalila et Dimna*, trans. A. Miquel, Paris, Klincksieck, 1980 (2nd ed.).
17 See *Die Lehrreden des Buddha aus der Angereihten Sammlung Anguttana-Nikāya*, aus dem Pāli übersetzt von Nyanatiloka, 2nd volume, *Book of the four things*, IV, 39, Cologne, Du Mont Schauberg, 1964, t. II, pp. 46–47.

animals into slavery is called into question, slavery itself as a social institution is considered legitimate, and with it, the right of the master to complain about a fugitive slave. On this point, the Brethren share the common opinion of their milieu and their time.[18]

Since no one can be at once party and judge, the case is brought before the tribunal of a being who is neither man nor animal: the king of the Jinn. That this trial is a fiction is only too clear. One, however, will note that it dramatizes an implicit response to an objection that had been raised since Antiquity, to wit: that a common law does not govern men and beasts.[19] Here, the plot assumes that common rules of right are shared by the three species of creatures. In any case, it is remarkable that the term "legitimacy" here finds its full meaning as a term of art, involving *lex/legis*, law.

The action unfolds over seven days: the king entertains his guests for three days before admitting them to his tribunal, and then the trial takes four days.[20] This framework of a week perhaps alludes to the chronological cycles that dominated the Brethren's vision of the world.[21] It will also play a role in the dénouement of the epistle that I am commenting on.

The first day of debates is taken up with a preliminary display of force between the men and a special category of animals, those that men have been able to domesticate. The men make much of the harmonious physical nature of their species, its upright posture, the acuity of their senses and intellect, which prove their

18 See R. Brunschvig, "'*Abd*," in *The Encyclopedia of Islam*, ed. C. E. Bosworth, E. van Donzel, B. Lewis and Ch. Pellat, Leyden, Brill, t. I, 1960, pp. 25a–41a.

19 See Plutarch, *De sollertia animalium*, 6 (964bc), *Moralia*, VI-1, op. cit., p. 24; and E. Kant, *Metaphysik der Sitten*, "Rechtslehre," "Einteilung," III, in *Werke*, ed. W. Weischedel, Darmstadt, Wissenschaftliche Buchgesellschaft, 1956, t. IV, p. 349.

20 *Animaux*, p. 205/159 (delay of three days, then 1ˢᵗ day), then 275/139 (2ⁿᵈ day), 291/159 (3ʳᵈ day), 337/221 (4ᵗʰ day).

21 See Ikhwan al-Safâ', *Les Révolutions et les Cycles. Épitres des Frères de la Pureté*, XXXVI, ed. and trans. G. de Callataÿ, Beyrouth, Al-Bouraq, and Louvain-la-Neuve, Bruylant-Academia, 1996.

superiority. The mule responds that all the animals have a body that perfectly suits their function. And the animals have finer senses than men.[22]

The domesticated animals renew their complaints against the harsh treatment humans inflict on them. The ass, the bull, the buck, the camel, the elephant, the horse, the mule, the pig, recall them in turn.[23] Then it is the turn of the hare. After a digression on the virtues and vices of the horse,[24] it is the ass and the bull that speak.

The presentation of the parties

The night that separates the first and second day takes on a particular importance in the unfolding of the plot. The three groups of actors come together in separate groups and decide on the course of action to take.

The king of the Jinn confers with his minister. What to do? To buy the animals from men would be too costly; to have them flee would be to create an implacable hostility between men and the Jinn. In any event, observes a sage, this animosity is already well established (we will return to this point).[25]

On their side, men put forth the most diverse opinions; thirty replies produce a cacophony of contradictory views and interests, which are defended unscrupulously.[26]

The animals themselves are divided into seven classes: quadrupeds (we would say, mammals), wild beasts, singing birds, winged insects, birds of prey, crawling animals, swimming ones.[27] The decision is made: the king of each of these categories must choose a representative whom he will send to the rhetorical combat.

22 *Animaux,* pp. 210–13/49–52; see also Porphyry, *DA,* III, 8, 3–5, pp. 162–63.
23 *Ibid.,* pp. 217–19/58–61.
24 *Ibid.,* pp. 220–21/61–63.
25 *Ibid.,* pp. 224–33/66–81.
26 *Ibid.,* pp. 234–37/81–86.
27 *Ibid.,* p. 238/87.

The lion, king of wild beasts, and his minister, the cheetah, successively dismiss the leopard, then the cheetah, the wolf, the fox, the weasel, the ape, the cat, the dog, the hyena, and the rat. After having recalled the qualities that a good ambassador ought to possess, the choice of the king falls on the jackal Kalilah, known from the famous fables of Ibn al-Muqaffa', their principal narrator (along with his brother Dimnah).[28]

The party of humanity is formed by "about seventy men," a number that should be significant because the Brethren emphasize it several times.[29] It doubtless is an echo of the Jewish idea of seventy or seventy-two nations of the world, to each one of which an angel is assigned, with the exception of Israel, for whom God does not assign a subordinate but assumes direct control.[30]

The dispute: the third day

The dispute opposes seven men who defend the right of the human race to dominate the animals. Their number is identical to that of the climates that divide the inhabited earth.[31]

The arguments they advance put into relief the advantages or qualities possessed by the human race:

(1) The prince of Rum (we would say, Byzantium) advances the sciences that man masters.[32]

The king (we would say, the queen) of the bees recalls that bees are as well organized and skillful as men. She praises the other insects: the ant, the grasshopper, the silkworm, the wasp.[33]

(2) Then a Bedouin intervenes who had not been present until then.

---

28 *Ibid.*, p. 244/95.
29 *Ibid.*, p. 205/41, 234/81, 278/143; "seventy two": p. 298/169.
30 See, for example, L. Ginzberg, *The Legends of the Jews*, Philadelphia, Jewish Publication Society of America, 1969, t. II, p. 214 ff.
31 *Animaux*, p. 300/171.
32 *Ibid.*, p. 310/183.
33 *Ibid.*, pp. 310–14/184–90.

The Syrian Christian who was, in contrast does not speak.[34] Why does he remain silent? And why would he be replaced by the other? These questions come to mind. The Bedouin recalls delicious foods and drink, comfortable clothing and furniture.[35] There is a paradox, and probably an intended irony, in hearing a Bedouin praise the pleasures of civilization, given that he leads a life of sand and lice (*raml wa-qaml*) as the proverb has it, and prefers his precarious nomadic existence to everything that urban life can offer.[36] In response, the nightingale argues that the good times are matched by the unhappiness that luxury brings. The good life that men extol is only obtained at the price of strenuous efforts.[37] It causes a thousand illnesses. The animals, on the other hand, enjoy it without having to work; they live without anxiety for tomorrow, or fear of thieves; they don't know the diseases, and their painful treatments, that only the domesticated animals among them know.[38]

(3) The Syrian Jew in attendance emphasizes that only men have religion.[39]

The nightingale responds that the possession of the religious sense is not the sole privilege of man. The animals praise God in their way, each in his own language. As for the acts of worship like fasts and sacrifices, they serve to expiate faults that the animals do not commit, to purify stains that they do not acquire. They can do without them.[40]

4) The Iraqi recalls the beauty of human clothing.[41]

---

34 *Ibid.*, p. 284/151.
35 *Ibid.*, pp. 315–16/191–92.
36 See M. Maimonides, *The Guide for the Perplexed*, I, 31. Translated with an Introduction and notes by Shlomo Pines, v. 1 (Chicago: University of Chicago Press, 2010).
37 *Animaux*, pp. 317–18/193–94.
38 *Ibid.*, pp. 319–20/195–96.
39 *Ibid.*, pp. 324/203–04.
40 *Ibid.*, pp. 324–29/204–?.
41 *Ibid.*, pp. 329–30/208/9.

The jackal Kalilah responds that a good portion of these advantages have in fact been stolen from the animals. How dare men extol their beautiful clothes when they only obtain them by despoiling the silkworm of his cocoon, mammals of their fur, and reptiles of their skin?[42]

Adam and Eve were originally covered by their hair. They lost this covering as a consequence of their sin, thus disclosing their nakedness.[43]

To an objection from the man who recalls the cruelty of wild beasts, Kalilah responds that if the beasts attack and devour living beings, this is because they are now deprived of the sustenance consisting in the flesh of animals who die a natural death. Furthermore, it is true that the beasts eat one another: but what is that in comparison to the wars that men wage against each other? Finally, the best of men—the ascetics, the hermits—do they not choose to retire from human company and live among the wild beasts?[44]

The dispute: the fourth day

(5) On the fourth day, the Persian advances that human life knows what we would call the division of labor: there are rulers, artisans, and intellectuals of all sorts.[45]

The parrot invokes the majority of animal species. They too are governed by leaders, with this difference from human societies: theirs do not ask for anything in return for their services. Animals, for example, raise their young without the hope of being supported by them in their old age.[46]

---

42 *Ibid.*, pp. 330–31/210; also see p. 321/199: the honey stolen from the bees. See Porphyry, *DA*, I, 21, 1–2, t. I, p. 57.
43 *Animaux*, pp. 332–33/212–14.
44 *Ibid.*, pp. 333–37/214–221.
45 *Ibid.*, p. 330–331/210; see also p. 321/199: the honey stolen from bees. See Porphyry, *DA*, I, 21, 1–2, t. I, p. 57.
46 *Ibid.*, pp. 339–41/222–26.

A sage among the Jinn interjects a development concerning kings and angels.[47]

The parrot resumes his discourse to deliver long couplets on the technical prowess of animals. He praises the skill of bees, of spiders, the silk worm, the swallow, the worm, the ostrich, the chicken, and recalls that while the little ones of humans need a longer period of maturation, the newly born of animals are from the start capable of supplying their needs.[48] The Brothers put in the mouth of the parrot a wide-ranging satire that attacks the different types of human intellectuals. Poets are the first target. Language, which is their pride, is not unique to man, because animals, even all creatures, possess it.[49] Astrologers are attacked at length and their claims refuted.[50] Then are passed in review philosophers, geometers, doctors, merchants, scribes, the readers of the Koran, jurists, cadis, and finally, caliphs.[51]

(6) The Indian argues from the great number of human beings, which is larger than that of animals. This gives him the opportunity for an enumeration of toponyms.[52]

The frog has no problem pointing out the vast diversity of animal species.[53]

One of the wise men of the Jinn ups the ante by adding that spiritual creatures, angels or demons, fill the spaces in the celestial spheres, which are immensely greater than everything the earth can hold.[54]

(7) The last to speak is a man from Hejaz, i.e., the region of the two holy cities. He was first presented as a native of the adjacent plane of Tihamah and a member of the tribe of Quraysh,

---

47 *Ibid.*, pp. 342–45/226–29.
48 *Ibid.*, pp. 345–47/229–34. One can see here the idea of "neoteny" which will later be theorized by Bolk and others.
49 *Ibid.*, p. 349/235.
50 *Ibid.*, pp. 349–55/236–46.
51 *Ibid.*, pp. 355–61/246–55.
52 *Ibid.*, pp. 329–330/267–269.
53 *Ibid.*, pp. 371–72/269–72.
54 *Ibid.*, pp. 372–74/272–75.

Mohammed's tribe.[55] He recalls that only man can attain the joys of paradise.[56]

The nightingale responds that man is also the only creature who can be condemned to infernal fire.[57]

However, there is one point on which men have a decisive advantage. It is not so much the ability to attain to a future life. It is rather immortality in general, a destiny animals cannot claim. The previous objection concerning the risk of damnation could have been decisive. It was the source of a perplexity among the men of the Kalâm, as one sees in a problem whose insoluble character was decisive in the intellectual development of al-Aš'ari. One can imagine the reproach that a condemned person would address to God: Why, instead of allowing the sinner to lead his life of sin which merited hell, why didn't you have him die at birth, or even better, why didn't you stop him from coming into the world at all?[58]

But the anguish of possible damnation was defused by the all-powerful intercession of Mohammed in favor of the community.[59] The Brothers thus associate themselves with the popular attempt aimed at calming anxiety before freedom and the possible consequences of choice, by letting it be understood that, in the final analysis, Islam guarantees paradise to all its adherents, no matter what their sins might be.[60]

---

55 *Ibid.*, p. 285/152.
56 *Ibid.*, p. 374/275.
57 *Ibid.*, pp. 374–75/276.
58 See M. Watt, *Islamic Philosophy and Theology*, Edinburgh, Edinburgh University Press, 1962, pp. 67–68 & 82; T. Nagel, *Die Festung des Glaubens, Triumph und Scheitern des islamischen Rationalismus im 11. Jahrhundert*, Munich, Beck, 1988, p. 114, and *Geschichte der islamischen Theologie. Von Mohammed bis zur Gegenwart*, Munich, Beck, 1994, pp. 145–46.
59 *Animaux*, p. 375–76/277.
60 See L. Gardet, *Dieu et la destinée de l'homme*, Paris, Vrin, 1967, pp. 311–14; T. Nagel, *Die Festung des Glaubens ...*, op. cit., pp. 17, 39, 99, and *Geschichte der islamischen Theologie ...*, op. cit., p. 146. *IBH*, p. 158 omits all mention of an intercession.

Now, for the first time the argument shuts the beaks of the animals and mouths of the Jinn who, being forbidden to enter paradise, have nothing to respond. The debate thus could have ended. However, it was precisely at this moment that the men, or rather humanity, play their last card, their absolute trump: the perfect human who combines all the highest qualities characterizing the different human groups, whether ethnic or religious.[61] It is in view of this august personage that the king of the Jinn pronounces his judgment in favor of man. However, is it forever? An earlier passage had left some hope open for the animals: they will only remain captive for a cycle.[62] This is because the Brethren had a theory concerning chronological cycles. In its light, a sort of apocatastasis and general deliverance had to occur, similar to the exodus from Egypt.

Moreover, the triumph of man will not be eternal. When the era of Adam and his descendants will have been accomplished, there will no longer be living things on the Earth, except for those God will have willed to leave here. This promise contains a profound meaning (*sirr*) that the Brethren say they already explained elsewhere.[63] This is a customary technique of esoteric writing, the "dispersion of knowledge" (*tabīd d al-'ilm*), a technique mentioned by the authors of the collection of alchemy writings of "Jâbir."[64] However, I have to confess that I have not been able to find the

61 *Animaux*, p. 376/278.
62 *Ibid.*, p. 233/80; *IBH*, p. 46.
63 *Ibid.*, p. 228/73. The Beyrouth text omits the restriction included in the Dieterici edition. *IBH* (p. 41) only translates the allusion to a deeper meaning.
64 See Jabir ibn Hayyân, "Le livre du glorieux," in *Essai sur l'histoire des idées scientifiques dans l'Islam*, t. I: *Textes choisis*, ed. P. Kraus, Cairo, El-Khandgi, 1935, pp. 115–16; trans. H. Corbin, in *Le Livre des sept statues*, Paris, L'Herne, 2003, pp. 183–84; see P. Kraus, *Jābir ibn Hayyān. Contribution à l'histoire des idées scientifiques dans l'Islam*, t. I: *Le Corpus des écrits jābiriens*, Cairo, IFAO, 1943, p. XXXII; in the modern period, Joseph de Maistre believed he found its presence in the work of Francis Bacon, see J. de Maistre, *Examen de la philosophie de Bacon*, Chap. XVI, in *Oeuvres complètes*, Lyon, Vitte, 1893, t. VI, pp. 323–24.

passage where the key would have been given; I find myself in good company, though.[65]

The solution

What is the meaning of this text? At the very end, the Brethren warn the reader against a superficial understanding which would only see in their story a tale for children.[66] But if they whet the reader's appetite by alluding to a profound meaning, they do not show their cards and reveal its content. At the beginning of the following epistle, the Brethren repeat that they have another purpose than explaining what distinguishes the different species of animals: "Our aim in this will not be lost on the wise, if one pays attention to what we said in the previous chapter in connection with monarchy and the angels."[67] They thus underline the importance of the preceding chapter and a specific passage. The wisest of the Jinn there begins by presenting an etymology of the word "king" (*malik*) derived from the word "angel" (*malak*).[68] He then sketches a cosmology according to which the universal rational human soul is the representative of God on Earth.[69] Finally, he recalls, more clearly than anywhere else in the same epistle, the esoteric character of the text and the necessity of hiding the secret meaning from the vulgar and the ignorant.[70]

The *General Epistle* (*Risāla ğāmi'a*) which presents itself as a work by the same authors, and which is thought to reveal certain

---

65 Neither the English translations of Goodman (*The Case of the Animals Versus Man Before the King of the Jinn* ... , op. cit., p. 72, and *Epistles of the Brethren of Purity* ... , op. cit., p. 133, note 105) nor the German translation of A. Giese (*Mensch und Tier vor dem König der Dschinnen*, Hamburg, Meiner, 1990, p. 34) say in what passage this promise is kept.

66 *Animaux*, p. 377/omitted.

67 *Épîtres*, II, 9 [23], t. II, p. 378.

68 *Animaux*, pp. 342–45/226–29.

69 *Ibid.*, p. 343/228.

70 *Ibid.*, pp. 343–44/omitted.

keys to the *Encyclopedia*, in fact contains a long passage that corresponds to the *Epistle of the animals*.[71] It conveys certain points that are not without their interest, but which can be found pretty much throughout the *Epistles*, for instance that man is a microcosm, that he is the vicar of God on the earth, that all the animals' characteristics are present in the human form.[72] On the other hand, it almost never addresses the dispute between the animals and men and only alludes to the context within which it is situated.[73] To the contrary, it concentrates on the nature of the Jinn; it develops the idea which is rather marginal in the *Epistle* of enmity between them and men.[74] But the *General Epistle* adds that this enmity can change itself into a friendship if, by piety, man raises himself above his condition, something that is not found in the text it claims to comment on.[75] All that however does not tell us much about the arguments of the two parties.

As for the content, the arguments that are exchanged are far from being new, and even the slightest research into the sources would no doubt yield a rich harvest of classical precedents. But one element seems to be original: the Brethren extricate themselves from the problem it addresses by "dislocating" it and "relocating" it in the form of an allegory. To be clearer: the domination of the human race over the animal species has become the image of the dominion of the superior man over his inferiors. This is probably a metaphor for the organization of the Ismailian sect: the *Epistles*, if they aren't simply the expression of that organization for purposes of propaganda, in any case have undergone its influence.[76]

---

71 *Ar-Risāla al-ǧāmi'a*, ed. M. Ġālib, Beyrouth, Dâr al-Andalus, 1984, pp. 155–221 [here *Générale*].
72 *Générale*, pp. 157, 158, 219–20.
73 *Ibid.*, p. 193.
74 *Ibid.*, pp. 204, 211–12; see *Animaux*, pp. 228–33/72–80.
75 *Générale*, pp. 212–14.
76 See S. Pines, "Shi'ite Terms and Conceptions in Judah Halevi's *Kuzari*" [1980], in *Studies in the History of Jewish Thought* (*The Collected works of S. P.*, t. V), ed. W. Z. Harvey and M. Idel, Jerusalem, Magnes Pres, 1997, pp. 219–305.

This idea was not without influence in history. One can even think that it never left the awareness of philosophers, who are always ready to consider themselves the indispensable salt of the earth, and to seek out some grand personage to whom they can be the all-powerful counselors.

A similar solution is found two centuries later with Maimonides. The Jewish thinker had no affection for the philosophical tendency represented by the Sincere Brethren.[77] However, he explains, as did they, the existence of vulgar or inferior human beings by the necessity of the superior man to have companions and servants.[78]

Many centuries later, Ernest Renan in one of his philosophical dialogues flirted with similar ideas. By the intermediary of one of the characters to whom he confided the task of expressing his boldest views, he explains that the vulgar serve by making the great man possible.[79]

At the dawn of extreme modernity, Nietzsche saw in the superman a "synthetic, recapitulating, justifying man" (*ein synthetischer, summirender, rechtfertigender Mensch*). Elsewhere, he characterized the supreme human as "the justification of the antithetical character of existence" (*die Rechtfertigung des Gegensatz-Charakters des Daseins*).[80] It is not impossible that the German philosopher recalled what his French colleague had written in the philosophical dialogues that Nietzsche had read.

---

77 Maimonides, *Lettre à Samuel Ibn Tibbon*, in *Letters and Essays of Moses Maimonides* [Hebrew and Arab], ed. I. Shaylat, Maaleh Adumin, Maaliyot Press, 1988, t. II, p. 552.

78 Maimonides, *Introduction au Commentaire de la Mishnah*, 7, in *Haqdam t ha-RaMBaM la-Mišnah*, ed. I. Shaylat, Jerusalem, Yeshiva "Birkat Moshe," 1992, p. 356.

79 E. Renan, *Dialogues philosophiques* [1876], 1, "Certitudes," in *Oeuvres complètes*, ed. H. Psichari, Paris, Calmann-Lévy, 1947, t. I, p. 576, then 3, "Rêves," pp. 610 & 618.

80 F. Nietzsche, fragment "Automne 1887," 10 [17], *KSA*, t. XII, p. 463 (*WzM*, # 866); 10 [111]; *ibid.*, p. 519 (*WzM*, # 881).

The lessons of the text

The same theme was reprised in the *Dispute of the Ass* composed circa 1417–18 by the Catalan Anselm Turmeda.[81] The author was perhaps influenced, directly or indirectly, by the Arab epistle. The *Dispute* is the work of a renegade, a defrocked Franciscan, who became a Muslim and lived in Tunisia, speaking and writing in Arabic. He thus could have had access to the *Epistles* of the Brethren, which had been in the Maghreb for several centuries, no doubt since Maslama al-Majriti, shortly before the year 1000. All the arguments advanced by man on his own behalf (here, by Anselm himself) are refuted by the animals, until the moment when man plays his trump card: in the Incarnation, God became man and not this or that animal. The argument is surprising, of course, coming from the pen of a convert to Islam, a religion for which the idea of the incarnation of God is a scandal. Nonetheless it points to a crucial problem: there must be an external perspective.

And the mention of paradise as the ultimate justification of the superiority of man and the decisive argument in his favor indicates a capital point that should be kept in mind. Historically speaking, it is interesting to note that the joys of paradise are the principal argument of the very first treatise on the dignity of man, that of Bartolomeo Facio.[82] This treatise is otherwise very inferior from a literary point of view, which is why Gianozzo Manetti felt the need to take up the theme and treat it in a more satisfactory way; he succeeded to the point that his work caused Facio's to be forgotten. And to be sure, if one judges Facio's little work according to purely aesthetic criteria, it is a real defect to have abandoned the proposed theme for the sake of an extremely prolix description of the joys of paradise.

81 Anselme Turmeda, *Dispute de l'âne*, ed. and trans. A. Llinarès, Paris, Vrin, 1984.
82 The little treatise of Facio was published in F. M. Sandeus, *De regibus Siciliae et Apuliae ...* , Hanover, 1611, pp. 149–68.

One, however, can still ask if underneath this formal inadequacy there still might be a profound truth concerning the matter itself. Is human life truly livable without the promise of an absolute joy?

Chapter V
The Word "Antihumanism":
Alexander Blok

Many centuries after the Sincere Brethren, at the time of the treatises on the dignity of man, the movement we call "humanism" was born. As we saw earlier, the term had to wait some years. But it did not even take a century for the contrary term, "antihumanism," to appear. I observed earlier that this word served as a convenient whipping boy to attack and that it is employed by those who want to promote a "humanism" without troubling to provide a foundation. In this vein, I will return to the polemical use to which the term has been put against Michel Foucault.[1]

Birth of a word

The word seems to be rather recent. The *Oxford English Dictionary* contains the adjective *anti-humanist* dating from 1904 (in the writings of William James), but it lacks the corresponding substantive. In Italian, *antiumanistico* is found in Benedetto Croce. German dictionaries know neither the adjective nor the substantive.[2]

---

1   See *supra*, p. 4 and *infra*, p. 89f.
2   *Trésor de la langue française*, s.v., t. I, p. 148a; *Oxford English Dictionary*, 2nd ed., t. I, p. 518a; *Grande dizionario della Lingua Italiana*, s.v., t. I, p. 529a; *Deutsches Wörterbuch*, III, 1, 1999, col. 17. (Since the original publication of this work, I found that Max Scheler employed the term *Antihumanismus* as early as 1912, in *Das Resentiment im Aufbau der Moralem* (*Gesammelte Werke*, Bern, Francke, t. 3, 1972, p. 110).)

In French, the term perhaps first appears in an essay by Jacques Maritain, *Humanisme intégral*. The Thomistic philosopher uses the term to characterize two positions that might appear to be diametrically opposed: the "brutal [soviet] atheism" and the Calvinist interpretation of Protestantism, which Karl Barth had just revived and which, according to Maritain, is equivalent to an "annihilation of man before God."[3]

However, the very first occurrence of the substantive is found in a Russian text seventeen years earlier (at least in the present state of my research). That is why I am going to look closely at this text, not only out of lexical curiosity, but also and above all because the antihumanist idea is treated there in a systematic fashion and receives particularly revealing treatment.

The text comes from the Russian lyric poet Alexander Blok (1880–1921).[4] In a Russia where the Bolsheviks have been in power for two years and where a civil war is raging, the poet committed himself to the service of the October Revolution. He publically affirmed his adherence in an impactful article, "The Intelligentsia and the Revolution," published in January 1918, which cost him many of his friends.[5]

On the 25th of March, 1919, Blok, who was working on finishing a Russian edition of the German poet Heinrich Heine, gave a conference on "Heine in Russia." In it he characterized the poet as being "antihumanist." He wrote:

3   J. Maritain, *Humanisme intégral. Problèmes temporels et spirituels d'une nouvelle chrétienté* [1936], chap. II, in *Oeuvres complètes*, Fribourg, Éditions universitaires, et Paris, Éditions Saint-Paul, t. VI, 1984, p. 370 & 373. On Maritain, see G. de Thieulloy, *Antihumanisme intégral? L'augustinisme de Jacques Maritain*, Paris, Téqui, 2006.
4   See A. Besançon, *Le Tsarévitch immolé. La symbolique de la loi dans la culture russe*, Paris, Plon, 1967, pp. 219–37. I cite: *Sobranie Sotchineniji*, Moscow and Leningrad, Éditions d'État de littérature d'art, 1962 [here = *SS*]; *Iskusstvo i Revolutsija*, Sovremmenik, 1979 [here = *AR*]; *Polnoie Sobranie Sotchineniji i picem*, Moscow, Nauka (in progress) [here = *PSSiP*]; *Oeuvres en prose (1906–1921)*, trans. J. Michaut, Lausanne, l'Âge d'homme, 1974 [here = *OP*].
5   A. Blok, "The Intelligentsia and the Revolution" [9 January 1918], *AR*, pp. 218–27; *SS*, t. VI, pp. 9–20; *OP*, pp. 322–32.

At his core, Heine is *antihumanist*. Never, it seems to me, has anyone expressed it more precisely; never has anyone expressed it like I would like to express it now, with conviction, while adding a *yes: yes, antihumanist*; and that is why he was always persecuted, always misunderstood, always watered down. Here is a great theme! I do not know if we will fix upon this terminology or if there will be another. But now, I cannot but note that the bell of *antihumanism [анмцгу манцзм]* resounds throughout the entire world, that we now find ourselves under this banner, a *crisis of humanism* clearly already exists; the world is cleansing itself, ridding itself of the trappings of the humanist civilization.[6]

The last sentence of the passage thus contains what is perhaps the very first appearance of the word "antihumanism" in a European language.

The "Silver Age," a new golden age of the apocalyptic

Since at least the turn of the century, all of Russia was obsessed with the apocalypse. External circumstances fed this obsession and in large part explain it. The Russo-Japanese War and the humiliating defeat to Japan, then in the same year the 1905 uprising, were traumatic. But even before that, the idea of a decline, of decadence, even the fear of collapse, were in the air, and events tended to confirm it after the fact, rather than cause it. Thus, in 1900 Vladimir Soloviev wrote shortly before his death his final text, the *Three Conversations*, which end with a *Short Tale of the Antichrist*.[7]

6   A. Blok, "Heine in Russia. On the Russian translations of Heine's poetry" [March 1919], in *SS*, t. VI, p. 125; *OP*, pp. 440–41. Underlined in the text.
7   V. Soloviev, *Trois Entretiens sur la guerre, la morale et la religion, suivis du Court Récit sur l'Antéchrist*, trans. B. Marchadier, Geneva,

The figure of the Antichrist evoked in the New Testament, especially in the Book of Revelation, had never been totally forgotten.[8] However, during that period it regained currency, as well as acquired a new credibility (and not only in Russia, as the example of the Englishman Robert Hugh Benson shows[9]). The image of the invasion of the armies of Gog and Magog, breaking down the walls that had confined them until then, received concrete plausibility after Japan's victory, reviving millennial memories of the Mongol invasion. It produced the figure of the "yellow threat," a phantasm since then often revived, even in comic books.[10]

In the face of this danger, the enigmatic figure of "what retains (or delays)" (*to katechōn*) or "the one who retains" (*ho katechōn*) (II *Thessalonians*, 2, 5–6) acquired a central place in the thought of several important thinkers.[11] He was an ambiguous figure because if he forestalls the horrors of the final catastrophe, he also delays the best of events, the glorious return of Christ.

Several Russian poets of the time, each in his own way, echoed a poem written in 1894 by Soloviev, but only published posthumously in 1905, in which Soloviev coined the word "panmongolism."[12] The danger returns, but in the form of a wish for a purifying destruction. The people who are its carriers are sometimes "them," and sometimes "us." It is in this context that one of the last great poems of Blok, "The Scythians," is situated, which has for its epigraph a verse from

Ad Solem, 2005; see the commentary of A. Besançon, *La Falsification du bien. Soloviev et Orwell*, Paris, Julliard, 1985, esp. pp. 90–101.

8   See J.-R. Armogathe, *l'Antéchrist à l'âge classique. Exégèse et politique*, Paris, Mille et Une Nuits, 2005.

9   R. H. Benson, *Lord of the World* [1907], South Bend, IN, St. Augustine's Press, 2001.

10 E. P. Jacobs, *Le Secret de l'espadon* [1946–1948], Brussels, Le Lombard, 1950.

11 See T. Paléologue, *Sous l'oeil du Grand Inquisiteur. Carl Schmitt et l'héritage de la théologie politique*, Paris, Cerf, 2004.

12 J. Deutsch Kornblatt, "Eschatology and Hope in Silver Age Thought," in G. M. Hamburg and R. A. Poole, *A History of Russian Philosophy (1830–1930). Faith, Reason, and the Defense of Human Dignity*, Cambridge University Press, 2010, pp. 285–301.

one of Soloviev's poems. It is the Russians who are identified with that ancient people and who ought to invade Europe, if its peoples refuse their heavy-handed friendship.

"The Collapse of humanism": sources and influences

The 7th of April in the same year (1919) that Blok had ventured, albeit in passing, the word "antihumanism" in connection with Heine, the poet gave a more systematic conference, which he repeated not long after: "The Collapse of humanism." (Крушение гуманизма)[13] Blok, who was to die two years later, was thirty-nine.[14] He started preparing the lecture the month before. In it he repeated the phrase that I cited earlier, the "bell of antihumanism."[15]

Blok borrows the bulk of his terminology from Richard Wagner, whose work *Opera and Drama* (1851) he mentions.[16] He also seems to have been struck by another of the musician's writings, *Art and Revolution* (1849), for which he wrote a preface not long before.[17]

He also alludes to Nietzsche when he mentions the phrase *gaia scienza*.[18] The German philosopher was read with great interest at the time in Russia, where he was mixed in all sorts of sauces, including a synthesis with Marxism.[19] Blok himself refers to Niet-

13 A. Blok, "The Collapse of humanism," in *AR*, pp. 288–308 [here = "Collapse"]; *SS*, t. VI, pp. 93–115; *OP*, pp. 414–32.
14 On the biographical circumstances, see A. Pyman, *The Life of Alexandr Blok*, t. II: *The Release of Harmony (1908–1921)*, Oxford University Press, 1980, pp. 338–41.
15 A. Blok, "Collapse," #7, p. 114; see also #3, p. 97.
16 *Ibid.*, # 5, p. 102; see also # 7, p. 114.
17 A. Blok, "Art and Revolution. On a book by Richard Wagner" [12 March 1918], *LR*, pp. 228–32; *SS*, t. VI, pp. 21–25; *OP*, pp. 333–37.
18 A. Blok, "Collapse," # 5, p. 299/106.
19 See G. L. Kline, "Nietzschean Marxism in Russia," in F. J. Adelmann, S.J. (ed.), *Demythologizing Marxism. A Series of Studies in Marxism*, Chestnut Hill, Boston College, and La Haye, Nijhoff, 1969, pp. 166–83; B. G. Rosenthal, *New Myth, New World. From Nietzsche to Stalinism*, University Park, The Pennsylvania University Press, 2002.

zsche from time to time, especially the Nietzsche of his first period, of *The Birth of Tragedy*, which speaks of an "Apollonian dream."[20]

To support his vision of the history of culture, Blok drew from the Swiss historian Jacob Honegger (1825–1896), who is largely forgotten today. He cites extensively from his work on the literature and civilization of the nineteenth century, which appeared in 1865, and which was translated into Russian in 1867.[21] In other writings he uses the book of this author as well.[22]

The portrait of history that Blok presents has similarities with those painted by several of his contemporaries. Thus Nicolas Berdyaev, in a text entitled "the End of the Renaissance" that appeared in the same year as Blok's conference, launched an attack on humanism, deemed to have culminated in atheism.[23]

One must recognize that the literary genre of the historical fresco played a role among Russian authors that it did not play elsewhere. The majority of Western essayists employed it as a simple summary of the acquisitions of historical research, which allowed a synoptic view, but was not necessarily connected with a value judgment. With the Russians, however, it took on the aspect of an apocalypse. The entire movement of Western culture is described as a series of fallings-away that increasingly depart from the truth, which is often thought to be preserved somewhere in the Russian popular soul. Slavophile historiography is full of this sort

---

20 A. Blok, "Element and culture" [December 1908], *AR*, p. 124; *SS*, t. V, p. 353; *PSSiP*, t. VIII, p. 92.

21 J. J. Honegger, *Literatur und Kultur des 19. Jahrhunderts in ihrer Entwicklung dargestellt*, Leipzig, Weber, 1865; cited #3, pp. 96–98, # 5, p. 104.

22 A. Blok, "Reflections on the poverty of our repertoire" [2 June–29 August 1918], # 1; *LR*, pp. 276 & 277; *SS*, t. VI, pp. 284–85; *OP*, pp. 405–07.

23 N. Berdyaev, "La Fin de la Renaissance. À propos de la crise contemporaine de la culture" [1919], in *Le Nouveau Moyen Âge*, trans. J.-C Marcadé and S. Siger, Lausanne, L'Âge d'Homme, 1985, pp. 15–47.

of broad-strokes reconstructions, which only have a tenuous relationship to historical truth.[24]

Culture and civilization

With Blok, the fundamental opposition is between culture and civilization, with the latter bearing a negative connotation. It does not yet appear in the text of 1908, which opposed "element" and "culture," this time with the latter bearing the negative connotation which "civilization" will later bear.

It was no doubt Thomas Mann who inaugurated this opposition when, in an article that appeared at the beginning of the Great War, he made use of the existence in German of two synonyms to distinguish German *Kultur* and Anglo-French *Zivilisation*—to the advantage of the former, to be sure.[25] Oswald Spengler extensively developed the theme in his *Decline of the West*; Blok, however, could not have read this book because it appeared a year after his death. Elsewhere Blok speaks of the "multimillennial lie of civilization."[26] If we need what belongs to culture, we have much less need of what is called "civilization."

Blok understands by "humanism" what the historians of culture call by this name, i.e., the movement that began with the Italian Renaissance. The classic authors of Weimar, Goethe and Schiller, are for Blok the most typical representatives of humanism. Humanism is essentially an individualism. Because of this, it was never able to penetrate the masses. When a new force entered the scene with the Reformation and the French Revolution, precisely mass movements, the crisis of humanism began.[27]

---

24 See A. Besançon, *Sainte Russie*, Paris, De Fallois, 2012, p. 91, n. 1.
25 T. Mann, "Gedanken im Kriege," *Essays*, t. I: *Frühlingsstorm (1893– 1918)*, ed. H. Kurzke and S. Stachorski, Frankfurt, Fischer, 1993, pp. 278–82, esp. p. 278.
26 A. Blok, "Art and Revolution," # 1, in *AR*, p. 228; *SS*, t. VI, p. 22; *OP*, p. 334.
27 A. Blok, "Collapse," # 6, p. 110; # 3, p. 99; # 2, p. 94.

But Blok does not fear "the revolt of the masses" that Ortega y Gasset will worry about ten years later.[28] On the contrary, for the Russian they have an entirely positive role.

> Civilized men are exhausted and have lost cultural integrity. In such epochs, it is the more vigorous barbarous masses who find themselves becoming, without even knowing it, the preservers of culture.[29]

Hence:

> The equilibrium between man and nature, between life and art, between science and music, between civilization and culture, is lost, this equilibrium by which the great humanistic movement lived and breathed. Humanism lost its style; style is rhythm; and losing its rhythm, humanism lost its integrity.[30]

"Integrity" here translates more less adequately the Russian *tselost'* (целость). The word constitutes one of the most abiding themes of Russian thought in the nineteenth century, especially among the slavophiles, ever since their coryphaeus Ivan Kireievski had forged it.[31] It was used to contrast the Russian character and the West. In doing so, one remained in the wake of the critique of "understanding" (*Verstand*) (itself typically Western ever since Schiller and Hegel), which dissects living reality and thus loses the beautiful harmony of the living organism. The slavophiles had read this critique in the Friedrich Schlegel of his Viennese maturity.[32]

28 José Ortega y Gasset, *La Rebelion de las masas*, Madrid, Revista de Occidente, 1929.
29 A. Blok, "Collapse", #3, p. 294/99.
30 *Ibid.* #4, p. 294/100.
31 See F. Rouleau, *Ivan Kireïevski et la naissance du slavophilisme*, Tournai and Paris, Brepols, 1990, pp. 175–80.
32 See F. Schlegel, *Philosophie des Lebens* [Vienne, 1828], in *Kritische F. S. Ausgabe*, ed. E. Behler *et alii*, Munich, Schöningh, t. X, 1969, pp. 1–307.

Music and element

Civilization is opposed to "the spirit of music." The expression echoes the title of Nietzsche's first book. From it Blok also borrowed the phrase "Apollonian dream," when he spoke of the "dream of culture, a great and fatal dream."[33]

"The secret and true cause of <these phenomena of decadence> is the spirit's abandonment of music; it alone possess the capacity to bind humanity to its creations."[34] Art is

> the voice of the element and an elementary force. Its unique destination, its meaning and its goal, pass by it; all the rest is a superstructure built upon it, the work of the ever restless hands of civilization.[35]

The nod to the Marxist vocabulary ("superstructure") is obvious. Blok hailed the Bolshevik revolution for his own reasons, which were not those of its leaders. The very last words of the article in which he made public his support for the revolution show that he saw in it a "music" that one needed to know how to hear.[36]

Blok makes great use of the word "element." The Russian word *stikhia* (стихия) comes straight from the Greek *stoicheia*, pronounced in the Byzantine manner. But while the Greek form is the plural of *stoicheon*, the Russian word is singular.[37] Now, Blok could hardly fail to detect in this word an echo (perfectly justified by etymology) of the word *stikh* (стих), which means "verse." The decomposition of things ends, as an essay of 1906 says, with a "chaotic

33 A. Blok, "On the realists" [May–June 1907], *SS*, t. V, p. 102; *PSSiP*, t. VII, 1997, p. 45; *OP*, p. 47.
34 A. Blok, "Collapse," # 5, p. 298/104–05.
35 *Ibid.*, #6, p. 302/109.
36 A. Blok, "The Intelligentsia and the Revolution," *SS*, t. VI, p. 20; *AR*, p. 227; *OP*, p. 332.
37 See M. Vasmer, *Russisches Etymologisches Wörterbuch*, Heidelberg, Winter, 1958, t. III, p. 15.

world in which everything is elemental."[38] But it is from such a world reduced to its simplest constituents that poetry can emerge as a new creation, in a way Baudelaire had already conceived.[39]

On the meaning of the word "element," one can read the essay of December 1908, "Element and Culture."[40] The text was written in response to an earthquake that had affected Sicily and Calabria and destroyed Messina, events which, very much like the Lisbon earthquake in 1755, remained symbolic of the destruction of European culture.[41]

Four years later, Blok noted in his journal his joy at hearing about the shipwreck of the Titanic: the ocean still existed![42] The element had taken its revenge. Blok again mentions the shipwreck of the gigantic passenger ship in an essay published at the end of the same year.[43] One should also note that the title of the essay that I am commenting on can also be translated as "The *Shipwreck* of humanism."

"What can preserve the spirit of music is the element to which it returns . . . that is, the people, the barbarous masses."[44] Blok cites some Latin words that he borrows from the Vulgate translation of Ecclesiastes: *Revertitur in terram suam* (*Qoheleht*, 12, 7). A few years before, in the account of a trip to Italy, he noted the same verse on 10 October, 1909.[45] In this way the adjective "barbarous" takes on a positive meaning.

38 A. Blok, "Evil days" [October 1906], # 3; "Russian literature"; *SS*, t. V, p. 81; *PSSiP*, t. VII, 2003, p. 30; *AR*, p. 33; *OP*, p. 32.

39 See my work *Image vagabonde. Essai sur l'imaginaire baudelarien*, Chatou, La Transparence, 2008, p. 58 ff.

40 A. Blok, "Element and culture," *AR*, pp. 121–30; *SS*, t. V, pp. 350–59; *OP*, pp. 190–98.

41 See, for example, "The Scythians," v. 12, in *Gedichtel* Смихомворенія, ed. A. Wanner, Frankfurt, Suhrkamp, p. 150.

42 A. Blok, *Journal*, 5 April 1912; SS, t. VII, p. 139.

43 A. Blok, "Art and the Press" [end of November–beginning of December 1912]; *SS*, t. V, p. 475; *PSSiP*, t. VIII, p. 155; *OP*, p. 277.

44 A. Blok, "Collapse," # 7, p. 304/111.

45 A. Blok, "Rays of culture," "Mute witnesses" [Oct 1909]; *LR*, p. 145; *SS*, t. V, p. 391; *OP*, p. 213.

Blok wishes to celebrate this return which frees from the customary melody of "the true, the good, the beautiful" currently submerging civilization, itself no longer a continent, but an archipelago.[46] This allusion to the transcendentals ("the true, the good, the beautiful") has in mind less their medieval version than the way in which they had been tailored to the taste of the day, the bourgeois spirit of Louis-Philippe, as found in a book by Victor Cousin.[47]

The selection of a new race

The reflections of the conference end on a blaring flourish:

> Man approaches the element. . . . Traits of an extraordinary cruelty [*жесмокосмь*] appear on him, as if they weren't humans but animals. [. . .] This dazzling sparkl is the sign of a change of race [*парода*]; the entire man has begun to move, he has awoken from the millennial dream of civilization; spirit, soul, and body are caught in a whirlwind. In the turbulence of a revolution in the spiritual, political and social <conditions>, which have their cosmic analogues, is produced a new selection [*амбор*], a new man is formed. Man, the "human" animal [*жцвомное гуманное*], the social animal, the moral animal, changes into an *artist*, to use Wagner's language.[48]

The conceptual language (race, selection) is marked by the Darwinism of the time.

One can tremble before this celebration of what will show itself to be in fact terribly inhuman, and in a way much more leaden and bloody than the rather irresponsible aestheticism of the poet of the *Scythians*,

46 A. Blok, "Collapse," # 7, pp. 305–06/112–13.
47 V. Cousin, *Du vrai, du beau et du bien*, Paris, Didier, 1853.
48 A. Blok, "Collapse," # 7, p. 114; I follow the reading of SS, *парода* ("race") and not the *прырода* ("nature") of AR.

and above all, *The Twelve*.[49] To be sure, the terms that for us have become the most offensive, "race" and "cruelty," need to be put in the context of the times. The first has nothing biological about it, but designates a human type in general. The second doubtlessly should be taken in the metaphorical sense that Nietzsche gave it, or later Artaud. They have been right, however, who noted that these terms in fact announced completely real horrors, upon which they conferred a certain legitimacy.[50]

Blok himself was not free from a somewhat morbid interest in destruction. In a youthful poem, he confesses himself "in love with annihilation" [в уничтожение влюбленный][51]; and he did not hesitate to court actual transgression. In his last years, a poem like *The Twelve* looks with dubious sympathy upon revolutionary soldiers looting, raping, and murdering.[52] A poem of August 29, 1914, already evoked an "incendiary Christ," in a clear allusion to the sect of Old Believers who immolated themselves in the flames.[53] And in *The Twelve*, to the reader's surprise—and the dissatisfaction of the Bolsheviks, including Trotsky who would have preferred to see Lenin in this role —the final verses reveal that it is this Christ who placed himself at the head of the band.

A text written in memory of August Strindberg mentions a "new sexual [подбор] selection."[54] It is deemed to reestablish the

49   See L. Heller and M. Niqueux, *Histoire de l'utopie en Russie*, Paris, PUF, 1995, p. 171.

50   See K. Motchulski, *Aleksandr Blok* [in Russian], Paris, YMCA Press, 1948, pp. 423–26; see also A. Pyman, *The Life of Aleksandr Blok*, t. II: *The Release of Harmony (1908–1921)*, *op. cit.*, p. 340.

51   A. Blok, Увнжу я, как будет погибать [26 June 1900], v. 6; in "Ante Lucem," Стихотворения Moscow, EKSMO, 2007, p. 39; *PSSiP*, t. III, 1997, p. 34.

52   See the very extensive commentary of S. Hackel, *The Poet and the Revolution. Aleksandr Blok's "The Twelve,"* Oxford, Clarendon Press, 1975.

53   A. Blok, Задебренные лесом кручи... [29 August 1914], in *La Patrie* (1907–1916); *PSSiP*, t. III, 1997, p. 168; see S. Hackel, *The Poet and the Revolution ...* , *op. cit.*, p. 119.

54   A. Blok, "To the memory of August Strindberg" [May 1912]; *SS*, t. V, p. 465; *PSSiP*, t. VIII, p. 149; *OP*, p. 271.

lost harmony between the masculine and feminine poles, hazy notions borrowed from Otto Weininger, who was then in vogue.

One finds a more peaceful vision of things in the last text that Blok delivered in public, a discourse that he read on the 10th of February, 1921—exactly forty years after Dostoyevsky—on the occasion of the death of Pushkin. Blok brings together element and culture in a more nuanced way: "The element carries in itself the seeds of culture."[55] This occurs at the cost of an operation that the poet again calls "selection." But it is culture itself that operates the selection.

As for the human being Blok, he participated in different literary commissions and gained a meager pittance from them. He died of a sickness aggravated by the famine and misery brought on by the civil war, after three years of poetic sterility. A conversation with Gorky, reported by the latter, allows one to think that the poet was aware of the responsibility of the intelligentsia:

> Once you have evoked the spirit of destruction and have summoned it from the dark, it is not honest or honorable to say: "It was not us who did that, it was *those* men over there." Bolshevism was the inevitable conclusion of all the work accomplished by the intelligentsia in the professorate, in the editorial offices, in underground plotting.[56]

The figure of the artist

The conference ends in this way:

> The movement of the "humane" civilization has been replaced by a new movement, itself also born of the spirit of music. [. . .] However, a new role for the

---

55 A. Blok, "On the mission of the poet" [Feb. 1921]; *AR*, p. 350; *SS*, t. VI, p. 161; *OP*, p 470.
56 Cited by A. Pyman, *The Life of Aleksandr Blok*, t. II: *The Release of Harmony (1908–1921), op. cit.*, p. 342.

person, a new human race, already declares itself in this movement. The goal of this movement is no longer the ethical, political or "humane" man, but *man, the artist*.[57]

Blok alludes to the traditional definitions of man and rejects them. Antihumanism consists in no longer defining man by what is human in him. The poet replaces the current definitions of man with a new specific difference, "artist." This is what constitutes a "new man." In the same way, at the very end of an article of March 12, 1918, Blok already mentioned a "new man, a new step in the direction of the artist."[58] The idea of the new man runs through all of Russian culture since Catherine II, and took on the most diverse forms before spreading to the rest of Europe, including German National Socialism.[59] Blok conceives this man above all as an artist.

Elsewhere he develops the implications of this term borrowed from Wagner's vocabulary:

> The entire artistic milieu until the present has been too little popular, too little elementary; it produced many artistic products, but it has not produced, and cannot produce, the *artist* [артист]—whom Wagner dreamed of, after having established this idea on an indestructible bond with the various revolutionary, popular, and elementary movements.[60]

Blok had to explain his use of the word during a discussion that followed the second reading of his conference before the Philosophical

57 A. Blok, "Collapse," # 7, p. 115.
58 A. Blok, "Art and Revolution," # 4; *SS*, t. VI, p. 25; *AR*, p. 232; *OP*, p. 337.
59 See the synthesis of D. Negro, *El Mito del hombre nuevo*, Madrid, Encuentro, 2009.
60 A. Blok, "Reflections on the poverty of our repertoire" [2 June–29 August 1918], # 4; *AR*, p. 282; *SS*, t. VI, pp. 290–91; *OP*, p. 411.

Society, the 16th of November, 1919, of which we possess the related notes:

> Out of prudence I used the word "artist" because I can't decide, I don't know how, I don't have the right, to use a greater word. I see that every human waste gives rise to a new being, I name <it> with a prudent word. But the phrase *the integral man* [человек цельний] is far from saying everything.[61]

The twice-invoked figure of the artist continues a long-term valorization of "creativity," which, paradoxically, has its roots in the period with which Blok wants to break, i.e., "humanism." From the practical point of view, since the Italians of the Renaissance, and from the perspective of theoretical reflection, since Rousseau, the "creative" artist has become the model of the human being who has remained intact, as Leo Strauss's profound observation noted.[62]

The image under the repainting

A passage that Blok did not publish allows us to see this more precisely. I translate it here because I have not found a French translation anywhere.

> Even if all of that is contestable and paradoxical, if the struggle whose final stage we are living through will not be called the struggle of humanism with antihumanism, of civilization against culture, of the "human, all too human" against music; in any case, one thing remains indubitable: that the goal of the new historical movement is no longer the aesthetic, or political, or humane human; these were mere masks in the past.

61 A. Blok, "Summary of the discussion," SS, t. VI, p. 462.
62 L. Strauss, *Natural Right and History*, The University of Chicago Press, 1953, p. 293.

The human face was darkened by the "languid brush" of civilization; now the "foreign colors" become "decrepit scales." However, for us it is still unusual and even terrifying to cast a glance on the unpainted face, the wild, uncivilized face, of the new man; only the spirit of music, to which the barbarian is closer than the civilized human being, assists us in recognizing and interpreting it.

Music is the voice of the masses.

To know oneself, to recognize oneself, to feel one lacks the ear, this would already be the greatest success of the Russian intelligentsia. In this way it would lose its self-satisfaction: self-satisfaction is the principal obstacle on the paths of music.[63]

In the central paragraph Blok plays on a famous little poem of Pushkin, *Renaissance*.[64] He borrows several words from it, and underlines the more literal citations from it by quotation marks. But he reverses the meaning of the poem, perhaps suggesting his own procedure by reversing the order of the adjective and the substantive. In Pushkin, it was about a barbarian when it comes to art who had covered up the *chef d'oeuvre* of a genius with his own artless strokes. By peeling them off, the process liberated the original beauty of the work. The poet opposes two qualities of art, one good, the other bad. One remains within the artificial, however, and the border passes between two of its levels.

For Blok, in contrast, the artificial covers over the natural. Thus he thinks less about Pushkin, even if he cites him, than Nietzsche, to whom he obviously refers with the words "human, all too human." The German philosopher had used the same metaphor of

---

63 A. Blok, "Unpublished fragment of the conference," 3, in *SS*, t. VI, p. 461.
64 Pushkin, Возрожде́ние[1819], in *Sotchinenija*, Paris, YMCA Press, 1991, p. 271.

a flattering color that covers over "the terrible original text *homo natura*."[65] For Blok, the barbarian no longer is the saboteur who ruins the painting, but the one who has the courage to confront the harsh truth which civilization has cowardly camouflaged.

Blok was a great lyrical poet, the greatest since Pushkin in the judgment of many knowledgeable critics. In contrast, he was not a philosopher of great stature. The ideas expressed in his essays, and in particular in "The Collapse of humanism," were those he borrowed from the atmosphere of the time. The aestheticizing antihumanism of Blok is not dissimilar to that of the Italian futurists before the Great War, or the German expressionists in its aftermath. However, for us the Russian poet has the interest of having named and formulated quite clearly a certain sensibility, to be sure one deeply rooted in the particular circumstances of the Great War and the October Revolution, but which remains a constant possibility of the human spirit.

---

65 F. Nietzsche, *Jenseits von Gut und Böse*, VII, # 230; *KSA*, t. V, p. 169.

Chapter VI
Contesting Humanism: Michel Foucault

The French philosopher and historian Michel Foucault (1926–1984) became famous with his book *Les Mots et les Choses* (1966), and especially by its last pages, where one finds the image of a human face which melts away like a sandcastle on the beach.[1] These words were so often repeated and wrongly interpreted that their author had to explain on several occasions what he meant.

At first, Foucault pretty much contented himself with saying that he had in view "humanism." His position was therefore styled an "antihumanism." Foucault himself highlighted it when he employed the phrase "horrible antihumanism" with mock stage fright; but he only mildly protested its use.[2] This contrasted starkly with the sarcasms that he always showered on the various hacks who styled him a "structuralist."[3] He did this however only from the late 1960s. Earlier texts displayed a more moderate way of taking his distance from, even a tacit acceptance of, this designation and the kinship it implied with other authors characterized by the same term.[4]

---

1   M. Foucault, *Les Mots et les Choses. Une archéologie des sciences humaines*, Paris, Gallimard, 1966 [here = *MC*], p. 398. [In English, *The Order of Things: An Archeology of the Human Sciences* (1970).]
2   M. Foucault, 54 [1968], *Dits et Écrits*, Paris, Gallimard, "Quarto," 2001 [here = *DE*], I, p. 679.
3   See, for example, M. Foucault, *L'Ordre du discours. Leçon inaugurale au Collège de France prononcée le 2 décembre 1970*, Paris, Gallimard, 1971, p. 72; 50 [1969], *DE*, I, p. 631; 72 [1970], p. 881; 83 [1970], p. 1001; 105 [1972], p. 1164; 109 [1972], p. 1241.
4   M. Foucault, 47 [1967], *DE*, I, p. 609.

"Humanism" and its contrary do not figure among the list of central concepts that the specialists in Foucault's thought have come up with (nor "man" or "anthropology," for that matter).[5] I therefore do not claim to penetrate to the very core of Foucault's thought in this chapter. It nonetheless seems to me worth the trouble to try to see as clearly as possible what the philosopher means when he uses the term, even in passing. In truth it constitutes a precious indicator of a state of mind that was not unique to him and which has not passed with him.

A death on paper

"The death of man" concerns first of all an event that pertains to the theory of science, and especially those sciences termed "the human sciences"; the book aims to present "an archeology" of the event. Foucault further specified it during a discussion held at the French Philosophical Society, and in particular to a question posed by Lucien Goldmann:

> The death of man is a theme that allows one to bring to light the way in which the concept of man has functioned in knowledge. [. . .] It doesn't mean that man is dead, it means, beginning with the theme—which doesn't originate with me and has been constantly repeated since the end of the nineteenth century—that man is dead (or that he is going to disappear, or that he will be replaced by the superman), to see how, according to what rules, the concept of man was formed and functioned.[6]

5   See the recent inventories: in French, J. Revel, *Dictionnaire Foucault*, Paris, Ellipses, 2007, and *Le Vocabulaire de Foucault*, Paris, Ellipses, 2009; in German: C. Kammler *et alii, Foucault Handbuch. Leben – Werke – Wirken*, IV, "Begriffe und Konzept," Stuttgart-Weimar, Metzler, 2008; M. Ruoff, *Foucault-Lexikon*, Paderborn, Fink, 2009 (2nd ed.).

6   M. Foucault, 69 [1969], *DE*, I, p. 845.

A text from the same year provides another precious clue:

> One shouldn't be particularly moved by the end of man: it is only a particular case, or if you wish, one of the more visible forms, of a much more general demise. I don't mean by that the death of God, but that of the subject, the Subject with a capital S, the subject as the origin and foundation of Knowledge, of Liberty, of Language, and of History.[7]

The death of man therefore indicates that one is aware that a concept has become useless, incapable of fulfilling its promises. Elsewhere, Foucault seems to identify the enemy with "the sovereignty of the subject, and the twin figures of anthropology and humanism," formulas that recur in a striking way in the essay on methodology that follows *Les Mots et les Choses*.[8] In this connection, however, one can note that the Foucault of the 1980s rather curiously ended by retrospectively rereading his entire oeuvre on the basis of the concept of "subject."

The revoking of the concept of man coincides with the following observation: everything is not given to consciousness.[9] In that way, the human is defined by consciousness.

Without always using the word "humanism," Foucault associates himself with the long-term movement of "the calling into question of the status of man, the status of the subject, of the privilege of man."[10] In this connection, he does not hesitate to reprise the legend, itself taken up and popularized by Freud, of the humiliation by successive decenterings that man has suffered since Copernicus, who expelled him from the center of the universe, then Darwin, who

7   M. Foucault, 68 [1969], *DE*, I, p. 816.
8   M. Foucault, *L'Archéologie du savoir*, Paris, Gallimard, 1969 [here = *Archéologie*], p. 22. "Humanisme," *ibid.*, pp. 26 & 266; "souveraineté du sujet," p. 272, see also p. 250; "souveraineté de la conscience," pp. 24 & 263.
9   M. Foucault, *Archéologie*, p. 274.
10 M. Foucault, 66 [1969], *DE*, I, p. 807.

dethroned him from the summit of the living, then psychoanalysis, which chased consciousness (and conscience) from his very soul.[11]

Beside the refined misunderstandings of the intellectuals, the crudest one of all was to take Foucault's declarations to mean the material extinction of man. The philosopher therefore held himself obliged to state clearly that he "absolutely had not wanted to say that man, as a living species or a social species, has disappeared from the planet."[12] This, as he himself began by noting, is obvious, and it would be unfair to impute to him such stupidity.

It remains, however, that this precision took away a good deal of the sharpness of the formulation, in fact it reduced it to a rather grandiloquent *façon de parler*. In this way we only have a not too serious literary death.

In contrast to, say, Günther Anders, whom I mentioned earlier, Foucault does not seem to have been very troubled by the possibility of an actual disappearance of man.[13] He devoted a great deal of his energy to social and political causes, for example, prison conditions. However, the three concrete factors that I earlier enumerated which are capable of bringing on the end of the human species do not seem to have attracted very much of his attention.[14]

In this way we find ourselves before a strategy of the banalization of experiences by their transposition into literature, the same strategy, as we will see, Foucault rued that it served as the loophole of Western humanism, which thus spared itself the task of addressing truly serious questions.[15]

The context

To understand Foucault's intention, one must begin by setting aside the context of the 1950s and 60s, in which he was formed and

11 M. Foucault, 81 [1970], *DE*, I, p. 968; nuances, following Koyré in 6 [1961], I, p. 198.
12 M. Foucault, 50 [1967], *DE*, I, p. 646.
13 See *supra*, pp. 34–38.
14 See *supra*, p. 23.
15 M. Foucault, 98 [1971], *DE*, I, p. 1095.

against which he reacted. On several occasions Foucault invoked "soft humanism," an expression that for him is redundant: "Upon reflection, I would say that "soft humanism" is a purely redundant formula, and that "humanism" implies in any case "softness."[16] He names a few whipping boys. For example, the Jesuit paleontologist Pierre Teilhard de Chardin, whom he never knew. Or Roger Garaudy, then in his communist period. He knew him personally and had his differences when they both taught philosophy at the University of Clermont-Ferrand, Foucault as an assistant, Garaudy as a professor.[17]

This humanism served equally well to justify Stalinism as well as Christian democracy, and would be "the little whore of all thought, of all morality, of all the politics, of the past twenty years."[18]

Jean-Paul Sartre is often cited as the type of thought from which Foucault sought to distinguish himself. For those of his generation who sought to make a place for themselves, it was necessary to distance themselves from Sartre, who dominated the intellectual world at the time. To contrast Foucault (or the alleged "structuralism" in its entirety) with Sartrean existentialism therefore became a common mode of classification, employed by Foucault himself, and especially by journalists. However (and this is strange), it doesn't appear that Foucault ever mentioned the conference Sartre gave in 1946 and which was published under the title, *Existentialism is a humanism*.

The case of Martin Heidegger provides the same sort of surprise. Foucault acknowledged the considerable influence that the

16 M. Foucault, 50 [1967], *DE*, I, p. 643. See also "marxisme mou, fade, humaniste," 54 [1968], p. 682. [Translator's note: the word "mou" could also be translated as "flabby."]
17 M. Foucault, 39 [1966], DE, I, p. 569; 54 [1968], p. 684, 686; 349 [1981], DE, II, pp. 1485–86; 362 [1982], p. 1601. On Roger Garaudy, see D. Eribon, *Michel Foucault*, Paris, Flammarion, 1989, p. 163; more details in D. Macey, *Michel Foucault*, trans. P.-E. Dauzat, Paris, Gallimard, 1994, pp. 129–30.
18 M. Foucault, 50 [1967], *DE*, I, pp. 644–45.

German thinker exercised on him.[19] However (and this is curious too), he does not ever seem to have cited his *Letter on Humanism*, which for his generation represented a foundational text that could not be ignored.

The true intellectual context for Foucault's reflections on anthropology and humanism is doubtless Kant's work; he himself summarized the relationship as follows: "Since Kant, the infinite is no longer given, there is only finitude, and it is in this sense that the Kantian critique bears with itself the possibility—or the peril—of an anthropology."[20]

Humanism: definitions

Foucault rarely defined this shameful humanism. A few passages proposed a sketch of a definition. Thus: "To simplify, humanism consists in wanting to change the ideological system without touching the institutions; reformism vis-à-vis institutions, without touching the ideological system."[21] Or again: "Humanism, at least on the political plane, could be defined as any attitude that thinks that the goal of politics is to produce happiness."[22] This prudent formulation is only a possible definition, however, not something that Foucault proposes as a thesis-statement; and on the other hand, it only bears upon a part of the field within which humanism operates.

In contrast, there is a text at the end of 1971 in which Foucault specifies what he means by the term "humanism." To my knowledge, this is the only text in which one finds an attempt to define it. This is why I will concentrate on it. Foucault provides the definition as a response to a question posed to him by a group of high schoolers to whom he had granted an interview. If Foucault is keen to define humanism, it is because he considers it the main adversary to defeat. He must take careful aim at it.

---

19 M. Foucault, 354 [1984], *DE*, II, p. 1522.
20 M. Foucault, 30 [1965], *DE*, I, p. 474; see also p. 467.
21 M. Foucault, 98 [1971], *DE*, I, p. 1099. I read "reformism" and not the "reformist" found in the text.
22 M. Foucault, 50, *DE*, I, p. 646.

The text is interesting for my purpose because it seems to me to bring together in anthropological form a good part of what I believe false, and even the contrary of the truth. In this way Foucault gives a definition of humanism that suits me perfectly, if only one changes its valence.

Here is the passage. I will present it in a broken-up way in order to facilitate its analysis. I also will add some words between <> to help more easily grasp the articulation of ideas.

> I understand by humanism the set of discourses by which Western man has been told: "Even if you do not exercise power, you can still be sovereign. Even better: the more that you renounce the exercise of power and the better you are subject to the one who imposed on you, the more you will be sovereign."
>
> Humanism is what successively invented these subject-sovereignties:
>
> <a> the soul (sovereign over the body, subject to God),
>
> <b> consciousness/conscience (sovereign in the order of judgment; subject to the order of the truth),
>
> <c> the individual (sovereign possessor of rights, subject to the laws of nature or the rules of society),
>
> <d> liberty as fundamental (inwardly sovereign, externally consenting and in accord with its destiny).
>
> In short, humanism is everything by which the West *blocked the desire for power*—forbade the desire for power, excluded the possibility of taking it.
>
> At the heart of humanism is the theory of the *subject* (in the dual sense of the word).

That is why the West rejects with so much insistence everything that could spring this bolt.

This bolt can be attacked in two ways.

<1> Either by a "desubjectification" of the will to power (i.e., by political struggle understood as class struggle),

<2> Or by the effort to destroy the subject as pseudo-sovereign (i.e., by cultural attack:

<a> the overcoming of taboos, of sexual limitations and divisions;

<b> the practice of communal existence;

<c> getting rid of inhibitions towards drugs;

<d> breaking down all the interdictions and boundaries by which normative individuality is constituted and directed).

Here I am thinking of all the experiences that our civilization has rejected, or admitted only in the element of literature.[23]

Historiography

Generally speaking, when Foucault seeks to determine the meaning of "humanism" he bases himself upon a rather personal or selective history. Others have noted that he exhibited the attitude of a great lord vis-à-vis historical facts, especially in his *Madness and Civilization: A History of Insanity in the Age of Reason*, which has been strongly criticized, in particular by Marcel Gauchet and

23 M. Foucault, 98, *DE,* I, pp. 1091–1104, citation pp. 1094–95.

Gladys Swain.[24] Nor did he hesitate to use his influence to prevent the publication of works that proposed another vision of the facts than his own.[25] The one who criticizes in theory the institutions of power can also in practice display craftiness when it is a question of employing them to his own advantage. This charge has been leveled against Pierre Bourdieu, for example.[26]

As for the historical location of humanism, Foucault gives various answers, which take us through three centuries. Thus one can read, in texts that are pretty much contemporaneous, the following affirmations:

> In the scientific discourses that man has formulated since the seventeenth century, during the course of the eighteenth century a new object appeared: "man." With "man," the possibility of constituting the human sciences was established. In addition, one saw the emergence of a species of ideology or a general philosophical theme: the imprescriptible value of man. [. . .] Man appeared as an object of possible scientific knowledge—the sciences of man—and at the same time as the being thanks to whom all knowledge is possible.[27]

But one also reads that humanism would be "the weightiest inheritance that comes to us from the nineteenth century."[28] And elsewhere, Foucault mentions "the anthropological and humanistic episode that we saw in the nineteenth century, when it was thought that the sciences of man would be at the same time man's libera-

---

24 M. Gauchet and G. Swain, *La Pratique de l'esprit humain. L'institution asilaire et la révolution démocratique*, Paris, Gallimard, 1980.

25 See D. Eribon, *Michel Foucault, op. cit.*, p. 168; D. Macey (*Michel Foucault, op. cit.*, p. 130) speaks of the "brutal exercise of power" (see also p. 433).

26 See M.-A. Lescourret, *Pierre Bourdieu. Vers une économie du bonheur*, Paris, Flammarion, 2008, p. 16.

27 M. Foucault, 50 [1967], *DE*, I, p. 635.

28 M. Foucault, 37 [1966], *DE*, I, p. 544.

tion, of human being in its fullness."[29] And stepping back a bit before answering a question concerning "the death of man," Foucault affirms that "the humanistic movement dates from *the end* of the nineteenth century."[30]

In any case, if Foucault is aware of the "great primacy of the subject, affirmed by western culture since the Renaissance," to my knowledge he nowhere mentions the treatises on the dignity of man, starting with Giannozzo Manetti (1453), that I mentioned above.[31] Nor the use of the term "humanism" taken in its current sense dating from the 1840s with Arnold Ruge, Proudhon, Marx.

In the sentence that follows the one where the emergence of humanism is placed at the end of the nineteenth century, we read that "man does not occupy any literary place" in "the cultures of the sixteenth, seventeenth, and eighteenth centuries," that "man himself is entirely absent."[32] I confess my perplexity. For this is exactly when Francis Bacon, at the beginning of the seventeenth century, albeit without naming it, defined what will later be called "anthropology": "I consider the examination of human nature in general, and in all its dimensions, as capable of being freed and constituting a science in itself." And what to make of Malebranche's sentence: "Of all the human sciences, the science of man is the most worthy of man," which will be echoed by the famous lines of Pope: "the proper study of mankind is man"?[33] To be sure, Foucault isn't unaware of the existence of major philosophical works in the modern period whose title indicates that they have man for their subject, and he cites them. However, according to him they occur before the parting of the waters represented by Kant's work. By posing the question of man, not as secondary vis-à-vis that of the infinite,

29 M. Foucault, 34 [1966], *DE*, I, p. 530.
30 M. Foucault, 39 [1966], *DE*, I, p. 568. My underscoring.
31 M. Foucault, 85 [1971], *DE*, I, p. 1034.
32 M. Foucault, 39 [1966], *DE*, I, p. 568.
33 F. Bacon, *The Advancement of Learning* [1605], II, IX, 1, *op. cit.,* pp. 123–24; N. Malebranche, *De la recherche de la vérité*, preface, in *Oeuvres*, ed. G. Rodis-Lewis, Paris, Gallimard, t. I, 1979, p. 13; A. Pope, *An Essay on Man*, 2nd letter, I, v. 2.

but by ensconcing himself in finitude, Kant made anthropology possible.[34] Here, though, we are only at the end of the eighteenth century.

The geographic location of humanism poses no fewer problems. In the text that I chose to examine here, it is a question of "western man," of "the West." Why this limitation? From what "other" does it distinguish itself? On the basis of what "East" would it separate itself and take on determinate contours? Where was what Foucault describes not the case? He speaks of "our civilization." Supposing the legitimacy of using the plural form of the term, would other civilizations exist that would not have the phenomena that Foucault describes here? China? Islam? The pre-Columbian civilizations? He mentions the East, "conceived as the origin, dreamed as the vertiginous point where various nostalgias and promises of return are born."[35] Foucault knows very well, and he says it explicitly, that there is something fantastic in this central point.

What is the subject of this humanist discourse? Who exactly is designated by "they said," "they closed"? One would like some names, if not of individuals, at least social groups or institutions.

The passage I reproduced is followed by an attempt to date the described phenomena. One of the young interlocutors suggests, "since the Renaissance?", an idea whose plausibility we just saw. But Foucault responds by invoking Roman law. It was "already a definition of individuality as subject-sovereignty." The owner is "the sole master of his property [. . .] while also obeying the set of laws that establish his property." Here we rediscover the same balancing act as in the four dimensions of humanism evoked above. And the same perplexity: how can what establishes be what one obeys? Here it refers to the transition from *de facto* possession to socially recognized property. I possess what I have power over, in the sense that I am physically able to defend it against another; on

34 M. Foucault, 30 [1965], *DE*, I, p. 474.
35 M. Foucault, *Histoire de la folie*, Paris, Plon, 1961, p. iv (4).

the other hand, I am the owner of what I can claim a right to in the language that connects me with the other members of the community.

Based on this model, Foucault interprets everything that *establishes* by reducing it to what *limits*.

An attempt at a critical reading of Foucault

Humanism as Foucault characterizes it occurs, as we saw, on four levels. Here I propose to address them in order and to show how the same operation I just critiqued takes place in each. He presents four powerful asyndetons, each of which must be understood to signify a concession, a "but . . . ."

(a) The soul "sovereign over the body." This perhaps is true for the Plato of the *Phaedo*,[36] but the accent is rather on the self-control of the soul, its superior part controlling the lower.[37] It is the same for Augustine, who includes in one of his definitions of the soul the ability to govern the body (*substantia quaedam rationis particeps, regendo corporis accommodata*[38]). But how to apply this characterization to Aristotle, who defines the soul as the entelechy ("perfection") of the body and who rejects everything implied by the image of the soul as the "pilot in a vessel"?[39]

"Subject to God?" Aristotle defines the soul without any connection to God or the gods. The divine is rather within, it is the intellect (*nous*) in it.[40] This intellect does, perhaps, come from without (*thurathen*).[41] But nothing suggests that it emanates from an external divine, and even less that it has a subordinate relation to it.

36 Plato, *Phaedo*, 80a.
37 Plato, *Republic*, IX, 589a–b.
38 St. Augustine, *De quantitate animae*, XIII, 22, *Bibliothèque augustinienne*, t. V, p. 272; *Cité de Dieu*, XIX, 27, ed. C. J. Perl, Paderborn, Schöningh, 1979, t. II, p. 582.
39 Aristotle, *De anima*, II, 1–3.
40 References in H. Bonitz, *Index aristotelicus*, 324a21–24.
41 Aristotle, *Generation of Animals*, II, 3, 736b27–28.

As for knowing if submission *to God* should be placed on the same plane as submission in general, I will examine that in the final section.

(b) The conscience as "sovereign in the order of judgment," "subject to the order of truth." In what sense is the word "order" understood here? An intrinsic arrangement, or a command? Or even "category, level, authority," as in Pascal's famous "three orders" (beauty; intelligence; grace)?

Conscience classically was conceived as a final authority, but as susceptible to education, in this way like taste, which could be formed. Thus St. Thomas did not shrink before paradox when he affirmed that there is a duty to obey one's conscience even if it is erroneous and counsels a sin. But according to Thomas, there is also a duty for the conscience not to remain closed in on itself and its fleeting impressions, but to instruct itself about what can solidly inform its choices.[42] In this formulation, this is the opposite of submission. It is a matter of liberating conscience from the constraints that come from one's humors, milieu, family, in short: everything that Kant calls "pathology."

And what does it mean to be *submitted* to the truth? In what sense can the truth, if it is what it claims to be, exercise constraint?

(c) The individual as "sovereign possessor of its rights," "subject to the laws of nature or the rules of society." First, one will note the surprising juxtaposition of "the laws of nature" and the "rules of society" connected by a simple "or," as if they belonged to the same category. This could have some meaning in the perspective of the Marxist critique of ideology: it would aim to dispel the illusion according to which the laws of a specific economic system, e.g., "capitalism," are taken as the eternal laws of human conduct. But this is not what Foucault says here.

Now, if the use of the term "law" is contestable because it is used metaphorically, there are real constants of nature that one

---

42 St. Thomas Aquinas, *Summa theologiae*, I, II, q. 19, aa. 5 & 6.

must respect if one simply wants to be able to act, or not act in vain. Plato already underscored this.[43] And Francis Bacon, who in contrast sees the ultimate aim of knowledge to be power, notes in a famous phrase that one cannot command nature except by first obeying it.[44]

The matter is also not clear in what concerns the "rules of society." It still would be a question of finding out whether the aforementioned "rules," which in fact have come from society and thus are not natural, would still be the expression of regulations by means of which the species as a natural reality provided the conditions for its survival.

(d) Fundamental liberty understood as "internally sovereign," "externally consented to and in accord with its destiny." The distribution of attitudes between the two terms of the division (interior and external) cannot fail to surprise. How would "consent" be something external?

The last formulation, "in accord with destiny," is used in an eminently positive sense by Nietzsche, whom Foucault follows even in the title given to the interview (assuming that the title was composed or agreed to by him). One question that merits being posed was not, unfortunately, because it brings to light the dialectic that is unleashed when one grants the highest value to "the exercise of power": in virtue of what logic does the theoretician of the will to power as the ultimate foundation of things arrive at characterizing his position as *amor fati*?

Operative concepts

Earlier, Foucault alluded to experiences that were suppressed in real life but which found refuge in literature. One would then need to reverse the movement and have them emigrate from the verbal element to enter, or reenter, the domain of concrete life. The allusion is, perhaps, to Sade. Or to authors whom Foucault indicates in

43 Plato, *Cratylus*, 387a.
44 F. Bacon, *Novum Organon*, I, # 129, *op. cit.*, p. 270.

other texts that they verged on madness.[45] With Hölderlin, Sade, Mallarmé, Roussel, Artaud, "the world of madness that had been put to the side starting in the seventeenth century, this festive world of madness suddenly irrupted in literature." That is why "there is a curious affinity between literature and madness."[46]

But the essential point is found in the idea that life is a place or site of experiences (unless it itself is one), this word, "experience," being taken in the sense of "experiment" in experimental science, of scientific experimentation. The idea is at least as old as Renan, even if it was John Stuart Mill who gave it currency.[47] The problem is that an experiment can go wrong, and can be inconclusive.

The central concept deemed to capture the essence of humanism is that of the "subject-sovereign." In itself, the formulation is inconsistent, because it qualifies the substantive with an adjective that is not compatible with it. In fact, since the definition given by Jean Bodin, the only thing that can rightfully call itself sovereign is an authority that is not limited by anything else, which judges in the final instance, and admits no other above it.[48] Now, we can either attribute this absurd formulation to the editor of the interview, or we can believe that it was a deliberately chosen oxymoron on Foucault's part; I believe the latter.

In either case, the entire passage witnesses to a stupefying inability to grasp the *constitutive* function of limits, which is expressed by the Greek term *horos*, which signifies at once "limit" and "definition." The word "taboo" used by Foucault also provides precious service at this point, as it has never failed to do since

45 M. Foucault, 222 [1978], *DE*, t. II, p. 490.
46 M. Foucault, 82 [1970], *DE*, I, p. 977, then 1000.
47 E. Renan, *L'Avenir de la science*, VIII, n. 68, in *Oeuvres complètes*, ed. H. Psichari, Paris, Calmann-Lévy, t. III, 1949, p. 1133; J. S. Mill, *On Liberty*, chap. III, in *Utilitarianism, Liberty and Representative Government*, ed. A. D. Lindsay, London, Dent (Everyman), 1968, p. 115.
48 Jean Bodin, *De la république*, I, 8; Hobbes, *Léviathan*, chap. XXX, p. 133.

Captain Cook brought it back from Tahiti in 1771. To use it to mean what needs to be "suppressed," "done away with," "overcome," obscures the difference between purely arbitrary rules and interdictions that are constitutive of humanity, for example, between genocide and wearing the tie of a university from which one did not graduate.

The great weakness of the passage, however, seems to me to reside in the use of the term "submission." It functions as a deliberately vague term, one that covers over relations of dependency that are quite different, even opposed.

From his first writings at the beginning of the '60s, Foucault considered finitude to be the fundamental concept of anthropology. In this passage from the beginning of the 1970s, however, he seems to reduce anthropology henceforth to the will to power. Human activity reduces itself to the exercise, and first to the taking, of power. These become the sole meanings and goals of existence. But this power, over what does it exercise itself exactly? Since such a power ought to rise above the Truth, and the laws of nature, our action risks being reduced to a purely illusory gesticulation.

In particular, it is not without apprehension that one reads in the course of the interview the list of means for the proposed "struggle." I remain perplexed before the "disinhibition with respect to drugs." As Foucault explains elsewhere, drugs for a Westerner constitute an "artificial madness" and would allow one "to recover in himself the intrinsic possibilities of madness."[49] But how can one assure that these possibilities don't turn into painful realities?

Death of God, death of man

Foucault names God in the first of the four fundamental ideas of humanism. Should one see in this decision to put God in first place a recognition of the decisive character of the choices that are made in this connection? In any event, it would be interesting to ask what

49 M. Foucault, 83 [1970], *DE*, I, p. 1001; then 50 [1967], p. 632.

idea Foucault had of God, and thus what his theology was.[50] As a matter of fact, there is no need to be a believer to have an idea of God. It can even happen that unbelievers allow themselves to describe the God in whom they do not believe while taking many fewer precautions than the theologians who confess their belief in Him.

Foucault understands the death of man as a logical consequence of the "death of God" announced by Nietzsche.[51] He thus takes up a connection that had been made before him, and he was perfectly aware that he was inserting himself in this tradition.[52]

Leon Bloy was perhaps the first to pose the thesis in all its radicality, writing in 1900: "It is quite permissible to ask if, truly, the Image is not as absent as the Prototype, and if there can be men in a society without God."[53] Closer to us, André Malraux has an imaginary Chinese say to a Westerner: "The absolute reality for you used to be God, then man; but *man is dead*, after God, and in anguish you seek someone to whom you might entrust his strange inheritance. Your little efforts at building a structure out of moderate nihilism do not seem to me destined for a long existence."[54]

The Russian philosopher Nicolas Berdyaev, three years before Malraux, had seen in the death of man not only something parallel to, if later than, the death of God, but like Bloy, as the logical and inevitable consequence of the latter: "The nature of humanism is itself revealed and unmasked, <this humanism> which at other

---

50 The recent work of P. Chevallier (*Foucault et le christianisme*, Paris, ENS Éditions, 2011), especially concentrates on the way in which Foucault understands the history of Christianity.

51 M. Foucault, 39 [1966], *DE*, I, p. 570; 42 [1966], p. 581; 55 [1968], p. 692; 69 [1969], p. 824; see also *MC*, p. 353.

52 M. Foucault, 69, *DE*, I, p. 845.

53 L. Bloy, *Le Fils de Louis XVI* [1900], chap. III, "L'absence de Dieu," in *Oeuvres*, ed. J. Bollery and J. Petit, Paris, Mercure de France, 1966, t. IV, pp. 98–103, citation p. 99.

54 A. Malraux, *La Tentation de l'Occident* [1926], Paris, LGF, "Le Livre de poche," 1976, p. 128.

periods seemed so innocent and sublime. If there is no God, there is no man either [Если нет Бога, то нет и человека]—behold what the experience of our times makes manifest."[55] It is interesting to note that Berdyaev declares himself, as much as Foucault (strange bedfellows!), desirous of seeing humanism come to an end. With this difference, though, that the Russian sees what he calls humanism as the direct cause of the death of God, then that of man as its paradoxical consequence. Foucault sees in the death of man the means of being done completely with humanism (as he conceives it).

It is out of the question that the absent, dead, that is, murdered, God could be replaced by anything whatsoever, and especially not by "Man." The idea was already expressed with perfect clarity in the last sentences of Foucault's introduction to his translation of Kant's *Anthropology*, the complementary thesis of 1961, but whose full text was not available until recently. Here are the sentences:

> The Nietzschean enterprise could be understood as the brakes finally being applied to the proliferation of inter-rogations concerning man. The death of God, did it not make manifest, in a double murder, that by putting an end to the absolute, at the same time man himself was killed? For man in his finitude is not separable from the infinite of which he is simultaneously the negation and the herald; it is in the death of man that the death of God is completed.[56]

It is probably as an echo of this declaration that one should read the final enigmatic words of the *Archeology of Knowledge*. Foucault hurls at his adversaries:

55 N. Berdyaev, Новое Средневековье. Размышленце о судьбе России ц Европы, Berlin, Obelisk, 1924; http://krotov.info/library/02_b/berdyaev/1924_21.html; in French: *Le Nouveau Moyen Âge*, *op. cit.*, p. 21.
56 E. Kant, *Anthropologie du point de vue pragmatique*, trans. M. Foucault, preceded by his "Introduction à l'*Anthropologie*," Paris, Vrin, 2008, pp. 11–79, citation p. 78.

It could very well be that you have killed God under the weight of all that you have said; but don't think that you, with everything you say, will make a man that will live any more than he.[57]

Foucault's theology

As for the connection between the death of God and the death of man, a particularly revealing passage from an interview states the underlying logic more precisely:

This disappearance of man at the very moment when one radically sought him does not entail that the human sciences are going to disappear, [...] but that the human sciences are now going to be exercised in a horizon that is not closed or defined by this humanism. Man will disappear from philosophy, not as an object of knowledge, but as a subject of liberty and of existence. Now, the human-subject [...] with his own conscience and his own liberty is fundamentally a sort of correlative image to God. The man of the nineteenth century is God incarnate in man. There was a sort of theologization of man, a redescent of God to earth, which caused the man of the nineteenth century in a certain way to theologize himself. When Feuerbach said: "One must recover on earth the treasures that have been lavished on the heavens," he placed in man's heart the treasures that he had previously ascribed to God. And Nietzsche is the one who at the same time that he denounced [sic] the death of God, denounced this divinized man about whom the nineteenth century had not ceased to dream; and when Nietzsche announced the coming of the superman, what he announced was not the arrival of a man who would resemble a God more than a

---

57 M. Foucault, *Archéologie*, p. 275.

man, what he announced was the coming of a man who would no longer have any rapport with this God whose image he continued to bear.[58]

This passage has the interest of placing itself at the origin of the modern sense of humanism as a concept, and even as a word, because mention is made of Feuerbach. In fact, even if the idea of a reclaiming by man of the goods "projected" by him onto God can be found earlier in the young Hegel, it was Feuerbach who gave it a systematic formulation and placed it at the center of his teaching.

The idea of man as the image of God is classical since *Genesis*. Its reversal by Voltaire ("If God created man in his image, man returned it to him in spades.") was simply a witticism, and did not go beyond the anthropomorphic critique as old as Xenophanes. Feuerbach took the formula seriously. The connection between the divine original and the human copy, the tie that entails that the death of God must necessarily entail that of man, is thus illumined, following the same logic we found in Bloy.

The way in which Foucault understands Nietzsche's idea of the superman seems entirely adequate to me. It is not a matter of putting man in God's place, but of acknowledging that this place remains, that is, it *must* remain empty, and of drawing out the full consequences by adopting an entirely "atheistic" way of life.

Two questions remain to clarify. On one hand, it would be interesting to know more precisely Foucault's idea of this God, in order to understand what sort of death man will suffer as a result. At one point Foucault provides an implicit characterization of "God" as "the center of a divine and absolute force, the summit of the scale formed by sacrality and its different

---

58 M. Foucault, 55 [1968], *DE*, I, p. 692. Other passages of the interview were disavowed, see 56, pp. 697–98. In any case, the text seems to have been quickly composed. For example, one will note that "this humanism" doesn't refer to anything before it, or the awkward use of the term "denounce."

values."[59] It would be worthwhile to retrace the genealogy of this god who is comprehended through the categories of force (not charity), of the sacred (not holiness), and of value (not the Good).

Here is a second question: Nietzsche also said that if each animal needs various conditions to exist, man requires one more: he must believe.[60] But what, beyond a striking formulation, does that mean? What if the absence of faith must eventually entail, via an entire series of mediations, the disappearance, this time not metaphorical but entirely real, of the human species?

The plenipotentiary

In the text I put at the center of this chapter, obedience to God is understood as submission, pure and simple. There are other ways of understanding it, though, for example the Stoic version according to which obedience to God is perfect liberty: *Deo parere libertas est*.[61] And what is true for "Athens" is true for "Jerusalem" as well: in *Exodus*, in the first of the ten words that are wrongly called "the ten commandments," the God of Israel presents himself as the liberator of his people (*Ex.*, 20, 2). The idea of the liberating character of obedience to God remained traditional in the three medieval religious traditions that brought together, each in its own way, the inheritance of the two symbolic cities.[62]

59 M. Foucault, 82 [1970], *DE*, I, p. 990.
60 F. Nietzsche, *Die fröliche Wissenschaft*, I, # 1, KSA, t. III, pp. 369–72.
61 Seneca, *De vita beata*, XV, 7, in *Dialogues*, t. II, ed. A. Bourgery, Paris, Les Belles Lettres, 1923, p. 19. An analogous paradox in connection with philosophy in *Lettres à Lucilius*, 8, 7, ed. L. D. Reynolds, Oxford, 1965, p. 16.
62 Boethius, *De consolatione philosophiae*, I, prose 5, ed. S. J. Tester, Cambridge (MA), Harvard University Press (Loeb), 1973, p. 162; Qušayr , *Risāla fi 'ilm al-tasawwuf*, II, # 29 ("Liberté"), ed. M. Zurayq and A. A. Baltji, Beyrouth, Dâr al- l, 1990, p. 219; Jehuda Halevi, *Kuzari*, V, 25, ed. D. H. Baneth and H. Ben Shammaï, Jerusalem, Magnes Press, 1977, p. 229.

As a result, the formula highlighted by Foucault could effectively serve, as he rightly believed, as the motto of European humanism. But everything depends on the conception one has of the God whom one obeys. According to that conception, obedience would represent either a mystification or a profound truth. And before that, everything depends on what "obedience" means, if it bears uniquely upon God.

The obedience to God functions in Foucault as the paradigm for obedience to every superior authority. That is why he names it first of the four modes of subject-sovereignty. One could agree with this intuition, but also correct it. There where the final object of obedience is God, this object is not a part of the world; on the contrary, it is the absolutely transcendent, the radically "other" to everything that one can obey. That is why it allows one to appeal from every other instance of authority that would claim power over me, even (and this is not the least important instance) if done in the name of "divinity." The term "obedience" is therefore imperfect, contestable, and is only used because of the lack of something better.

In any case, obedience to God cannot consist in sacrificing one's interest, desire (or whatsoever), in favor of God's. Because God is God it is simply impossible to cause him any harm, for example by disobeying him. The sole harm or injury that man can do is to himself.[63] What must be sacrificed is, if I may emphasize the prefixes, un-interesting or un-desirable. And one learns to do without them for the sake of what, or Who, constitutes, both for interest and desire, not so much an object but the infinite *field* in which they can exercise themselves fully.

The humanism that Foucault attacks rests on the contradictory concept of a "subject-sovereignty." In face of it, I would like to take up the paradox, but turn it on its head. To do so, I need to introduce the concept of man as *plenipotentiary*. This means: invested with a task, and thus granted full powers that allow him to fulfill it, but at the same time responsible for its execution.

---

63 See St. Thomas Aquinas, *Summa contra Gentiles*, III, 122, # 2948, ed. C. Pera, Turin, Marietti, 1961, t. III, p. 181b.

As for the conception of God that is in the background of Foucault's text, it seems to me that it is nothing but the archaic representation from which the Bible broke in decisive fashion. The biblical God affirms what is, and among that, man. We will see this, and how, in what follows.

Chapter VII
The Legitimacy of Modern Times?
The Case of Hans Blumenberg

My title and the underlying concern of the entire work are an allusion to the work which is probably the *chef d'oeuvre* of Hans Blumenberg (1920–1996), *La Legitimité des Temps modernes*.[1] I would like to justify this praise by entering into dialogue with this German philosopher, whose voluminous oeuvre continues to appear posthumously in Germany. In France, it is beginning to be translated, but it is still too little known. His method is that of the history of ideas, built on a staggering erudition, in particular in areas that philosophers do not often visit, the Fathers of the Church, for example.

Blumenberg's central book is a reflection on the nature of Modern Times. According to conventional historiography, these began with the age of "humanism." For Blumenberg this is not a mere coincidence. The connection is essential inasmuch as modernity, according to him, as well as the thinkers he evokes from the Renaissance to the Enlightenment and beyond, defines itself by the "self-affirmation of man." In this way my title is, at bottom, the same as Blumenberg's.

Modern Times as an epoch

Blumenberg understands Modern Times more profoundly than many of its advocates, but he still places himself in their wake, in

---

1 H. Blumenberg, *Die Legitimität der Neuzeit*, Frankfurt, Suhrkamp, 1988 [here = LN]. [In English, *The Legitimacy of the Modern Age*.]

the way they understand themselves. This fact suggests a preliminary thought: as Marx recalled, one doesn't judge an epoch, any more than a person, by the image they make of themselves.[2] I will return to this.

Be that as it may, Modern Times understand themselves as a rupture vis-à-vis a preceding period. With them, the very meaning of the adjective "modern" changes. Before, the term was relative and designated what was more recent than what preceded it; it became absolute and named what tore itself decisively away from a past in order to establish itself irrevocably in its own, and definitive, reality. One sees the paradox: the era of progress begins with the definitive halting of something.

This previous epoch, Modern Times call "the Middle Ages." The passage from the Middle Ages to Modern Times should not be placed on the same plane as the previous turning-point periods that we customarily use to divide history's course. This is especially true if one compares the end of the Middle Ages to their beginning, the end of Antiquity. In fact, only the transition to Modernity was not simply undergone, but was consciously willed.

> In contrast to the Middle Ages, the modern period did not exist before the moment of its self-declaration. The latter is not its engine, but it has constant need of it to organize itself.[3]

To be modern is to want to be modern, and to know oneself as such.

It is because the passage to Modernity is a choice, that one can pose the question of its legitimacy: by what right can one claim to "be epoch-making," to introduce a rupture in the unbroken continuity of history?

---

2 K. Marx, *Zur Kritik der politischen Ökonomie* [1859] preface, in *Werke*, Berlin, Dietz, 1961, t. XIII, p. 9.
3 H. Blumenberg, *LN*, p. 543.

The problem of legitimacy is certainly connected with the concept of "epoch" itself. Only the modern period understood itself as an epoch, and by that fact even created the other epochs. The problem is latent in the ambition of Modern Times to effect a radical rupture with Tradition, and in the disproportion between this ambition and the reality of history, which can never begin from zero. Like all the political and historical problems of legitimacy, that of Modern Times emerges across discontinuity, it being understood that it is immaterial whether this discontinuity is fictional or real. They themselves claimed this discontinuity vis-à-vis the Middle Ages.[4]

Blumenberg understands the passage to Modern Times as they understood themselves, i.e., as a departure from the Middle Ages. For him, this decision is not the result of an arbitrary decision, of a capricious will simply not to do what was done until then. Rather, it was a necessary process, which imposed itself upon the minds of those who were its most self-conscious agents. This necessity was the consequence of the failure of the Middle Ages and the solutions it proposed. Thus, it was the Middle Ages themselves that rendered the transition to other solutions necessary. In arguing this way, Blumenberg justifies the said transition.

Among other things, this is to run counter to another view which began with the Romantics, then later Neothomism, which saw in this the result of a betrayal, a fall, even an "original sin of thought." Above all, Blumenberg attacks the idea according to which Modernity would rest upon a "secularization" of thoughts issued from the Christian Middle Ages. This process would be analogous to the way in which the goods of the Church, in violation of all law, were purely and simply *stolen* by temporal sovereigns, in the England of Henry VIII, in the Austria of Josephism, in revolutionary France, and the Germany

4   *Ibid.*, p. 129; see also p. 537.

of Napoleon's time. The parallel was suggested, perhaps for the first time, by Wilhelm Dilthey, and has known remarkable success ever since.[5]

One can also note that this reading of history is an updating of another "grand narrative" which was much more influential, and at the service of more powerful interests that made it quasi-obligatory, which is the vision that the Enlightenment, then all the regimes that based themselves upon it, constructed of history, a "left" and "progressive" vision that the English historian Herbert Butterfield called "the Whig interpretation of history."[6]

Badly refuted Gnosticism

Blumenberg sees in the Middle Ages an unsuccessful response to the Gnostic temptation. As we know, Gnosticism is a sensibility common to rather different groups, and appeared towards the second century A. D. at the margins of Judaism and Christianity. It maintains that nature is evil, that it wishes ill to man, who would have fallen from another, superior, world. The German philosopher Hans Jonas would perhaps have been the first, in the 1930s, to have considered it philosophically, making use of Heideggerian categories.[7] Blumenberg's reading of Gnostic texts is the same as Jonas's.

Another philosopher, Eric Voegelin, saw in the project of Modern Times, and above all in its revolutions, a vast resurgence of

---

5   W. Dilthey, "Auffassung und Analyse des Menschen im *15. und 16. Jahrhundert*" [1893], in *Weltanschauung und Analyse des Menschen seit Renaissance und Reformation. Abhandlungen zur Geschichte der Philosophie und Religion* (Gesammelte Schriften, II), Leipzig and Berlin, Teubner, 1923, p. 19. Blumenberg, curiously, does not refer to the passage.

6   H. Butterfield, *The Whig Interpretation of History*, London, Bell, 1931; see my work *Au moyen du Moyen Âge ... , op. cit.*, pp. 39–44.

7   H. Jonas, *Gnosis und spätantiker Geist*, I: *Die mythologische Gnosis*, Göttingen, Vandenhoeck & Ruprecht, 1954 (2nd ed.).

Gnostic thought.[8] Blumenberg too is among those philosophers who see in Gnosticism one of the fundamental solutions offered to the enigma of the world, and he returns several times to the theme.[9] But he responds to Voegelin that Modernity, far from being a return to Gnosticism, is to the contrary an effort to exorcise it. It would have been rendered necessary by the failure of the Middle Ages to fulfill this task by furnishing a credible alternative to the Gnostic temptation.

> The thesis we want to maintain here takes up again the affirmation of a relation between Modern Times and Gnosticism, but in the reverse: Modern Times are the overcoming of Gnosticism. This supposes that the overcoming of Gnosticism did not succeed at the beginning of the Middle Ages. It implies that the Middle Ages, as a structure of meaning that covers several centuries, emerged from the conflict with Gnosticism at the end of Antiquity and the beginning of Christianity, and that the unity of its systematic will can be grasped beginning from an understanding of the Gnostic counterposition.[10]

According to Blumenberg, Gnosticism itself was born of a certain failure of Christianity. It was made inevitable by the delay of the *parousia*, the second coming of Christ. Once this eschatological crisis had passed, and the hope of the first Christians was disappointed, Christianity found itself with a contradiction between the God of the end of time and the God of the course of history. The incorporation of the Stoic idea of Providence into Christianity already witnessed to this,

8 E. Voegelin, *The New Science of Politics. An introduction*, Chicago, The University of Chicago Press, 1952, especially chapter IV: "Gnosticism—The nature of Modernity."

9 See H. Blumenberg, *Die Lesbarkeit der Welt*, Frankfurt, Suhrkamp, 1986, pp. 34–35; *Arbeit am Mythos*, Francfort, Suhrkamp, 1986, pp. 197–234; *Höhlenausgänge*, Frankfurt, Suhrkamp, 1989, pp. 225–34.

10 H. Blumenberg, *LN*, p. 138.

because the integration of Stoic providence into Christianity was already an act of secularization for the sake of a history that was no longer viewed eschatologically, or at least no longer needed to be [divinely] settled. The eschatological God of the end of history cannot at the same time be the one who manifests himself in history and proposes himself as a guardian.[11]

Supposing two gods, Gnosticism resolved the problem in its own way: the Creator is not the Savior, the Savior frees us from the world that the Creator either botched or constructed as a snare destined to hold us captive.

Orthodox Christianity responded with the affirmation of the creation of the world by a God of goodness. By the same token, it took up the "pagan" idea of the world as beautiful order, as a *kosmos*:

> The formation of the Middle Ages cannot be understood except as an effort to definitively protect oneself against the Gnostic syndrome. To save the world, as Creation, from the negation of its demiurgic origins, and to save its ancient dignity as a cosmos in the heart of the Christian system, this was the essential task accomplished by St. Augustine, the first scholastic.[12]

For Blumenberg, this synthesis of ancient cosmology and the Christian message is not tenable. In saying this, he presupposes the view according to which the Christian movement, and before that Jesus himself, can be reduced to the proclamation of the imminent end of the world. In so doing, he takes up the way of looking at things of Albert Schweitzer and his disciple, Martin Werner, whom he cites.[13] More broadly, he follows a good number of the

11 *Ibid.*, p. 41.
12 *Ibid.*, p. 143; see also p. 205.
13 *Ibid.*, pp. 54 and 142.

theologians of his generation, especially Protestants, who are now somewhat forgotten.

If the essence of Jesus's message is found in the eschatological announcement, it is difficult not to agree with the Swiss theologian Franz Overbeck, a friend of Nietzsche. For him, Christianity emerged from a betrayal of itself, in that it wished to make possible a world that denies it.[14] But the question to ask is if primitive Christian experience is understood completely and adequately by a *temporal* interpretation of the "nearness of the kingdom of God" announced by Jesus. To be sure, this interpretation is indeed found in the New Testament. But if, to the contrary, the fundamental idea is an intervention by God *in person*, his nearness could be understood just as legitimately in the idea of incarnation, and Jesus would be "the Kingdom himself" (*autobasileia*) of which Origen spoke.[15] In that case, the chronological question would lose all, or part, of its relevance.

The necessity of the modern enterprise

Blumenberg does not provide a formal definition of Modernity. But his view is clear: what is modern is above all the project of the conquest of nature, pursued by the application of mathematical physics to the elaboration of a technology that allows one to control it. The famous phrase of Descartes, "to become as masters and possessors of nature," is crucial here.[16] Now—and this is the entire problem—such an application of the knowledge of nature is not at all obvious. Historians of science and technology such as Joseph

14 *Ibid.*, p. 132, and F. Overbeck, *Über die Christlichkeit unserer heutigen Theologie* [1873], Darmstadt, Wissenschaftliche Buchgesellschaft, 1963, pp. 33–34.
15 Origène, *Commentaire de l'Évangile selon Matthieu*, XIV, 7 (on Matthew 18, 23), ed. E. Klostermann (GCS 40), Leipzig, Hinrich, 1935, p. 289; and see H. U. von Balthasar, *Zuerst Gottes Reich. Zwei Skizzen zur biblischen Naherwartung*, Zurich *et alii*, Benziger, 1966.
16 H. Blumenberg, *LN*, pp. 206 and 662; R. Descartes, *Discours de la méthode*, in *Oeuvres*, *op. cit.*, t. VI, p. 62.

Needham or Alexandre Koyré already asked why it appeared in the Europe of the seventeenth century and not, for example, in the China of the warring states, or Hellenistic Greece, or even the Islam of Iraq or Andalusia (since the Muslim mentality was not as resistant to technology as people sometime think[17]).

The Greeks seem to have conceived, or at least dreamed, of the idea of a technological improvement of nature.[18] But they did not seek to realize it. For its part, the Jewish idea of *tiqq n ha-' lam* (literally: the reparation of the world) was not originally, in the *Mishnah*, a conquest of nature, but a simple arrangement of legal means aiming at facilitating human life.[19] When the notion was reinterpreted by the Kabbalah, the lower world is only changed indirectly, by events occurring in the upper world and brought to the lower world by theurgic practices.[20] In this connection, it is appropriate to recall how the idea of "changing the world" comes from magic, and how technology was first of all thought by means of magical categories, for example by Francis Bacon.[21]

On the other hand, one could have expected other results from natural science than the domination of nature, and history has provided several examples. Thus, first of all, Epicurus conceived of a physics that had for its essential goal peace of the soul (*ataraxia*).[22] Hence the extreme importance of the study of Epicureanism, to which Blumenberg devotes a great deal of attention.[23] It is

17 See J. van Ess, "*Fatum Mahumetanum.* Schicksal und Freiheit im Islam," in *Schicksal? Grenzen der Machbarkeit. Ein Symposion*, Munich, DTV, 1977, pp. 26–50, especially pp. 41–42.
18 See Empedocles, *DK* 31 B 111, and compare with Xenophon, *Memorabilia*, I, 1, 15, cited by H. Blumenberg, *LN*, p. 282.
19 Mishnah, *Gittin*, IV, 2, 34b.
20 On this there is much to be gleaned from the book by M. Idel, *Golem* (Albany, NY: State University of New York Press, 1990).
21 F. Bacon, *De augmentis scientiarum*, III, 5, in *The Works of F. B.*, ed. J. Spedding and R. L. Ellis, London, Longman, t. I, 1858, p. 571.
22 Épicure, *Lettre à Pythoclès*, Diogenes Laertius X, # 85; *Kuriai Doxai*, XI, DL X, # 142.
23 H. Blumenberg, *LN*, p. 171 ff. and, again, p. 303 ff.; *Höhlenausgänge, op. cit.*, 334 ff.

conducted in the light of a fundamental question: why is the Epicurean attitude no longer possible? Why does the conquest of nature, and not simply disinterest in its regard, seem to be the only means of assuring the peace of the soul?

Here I have to pose a question: Is Blumenberg right to make Epicureanism a form of thought, even the characteristic thought, of *late* Antiquity? He has to do so if he wants to put in parallel the two conflicts by which one entered the Middle Ages and then left it.[24] But here the historian has to recall that Epicureanism had been losing steam for quite a while and had hardly any adherents after the third century. And, on the other hand, what to make of the Neoplatonism which in fact dominated late Antiquity? Perhaps Blumenberg could have reserved the largest part for it. The hero who too quickly believed that he triumphed over both Gnosticism and Epicureanism—was it Christianity, or a Christianity mixed with Neoplatonism (although not without conflicts)?[25] Neoplatonists and Christians had Gnosticism as a common enemy, and the rabbis of the Talmud for allies.[26]

Reaction to the absolutism of the nominalists

According to Blumenberg, Modernity came from the desire and the necessity of sheltering man from a theological absolutism, itself issued from an insufficiently exorcized Gnosticism.

> The Gnosticism that was not overcome but only transposed, returned under the figure of the hidden God and his incomprehensible absolute sovereignty.[27]

24 H. Blumenberg, *LN*, p. 205; and see the entire second part, chap. III, pp. 159–204.

25 See E. von Ivánka, *Plato Christianus. Uebernahme und Umgestaltung des Platonismus durch die Väter.* Einsiedeln, Johannes Verlag, 1964.

26 See G. G. Stroumsa, "Haq-qirbah han-nistereth: aboth hak-Keneisiya we HAZAL," *Mehqarey Yerushalayim be-Makhsheveth Israel*, 2 (1982), pp. 170–75; my translation can be found in *Communio*, vol. XXIV-2, n. 142, March-April 1999, pp. 35–44.

27 H. Blumenberg, *LN*, p. 149.

It was this absolutism that barred the route that could have led back to Epicureanism. We can no longer adopt an attitude of disinterest towards the world like the gods of Epicurus who spend a peaceful eternity in the interstices of the world and leave us in peace in ours. The God of theological absolutism occupies himself with the world and does not leave us alone in tranquility. According to Blumenberg, this theological absolutism attained its peak in the fourteenth century with the thinkers brought together under the name of Nominalists. For them, words are only tokens, mere "names" that do not grant access to reality, and especially that of God, who is in fact totally unknowable. They therefore conceive of Him as an absolute sovereign, pure unpredictable will, capable of giving things whatever appearance He wishes, which do not necessarily correspond to the truth.

In this way, nominalism seals the end of the world conceived, as by the ancients, as a *kosmos*:

> The abandonment of the ancient cosmos was consummated the moment when the distinction between power and act no longer corresponded to the distinction between reason and will, or when the act of the divine will no longer only related to the world's existence, but also to the universe of truths which have their validity in the midst of the world.[28]

At once, man finds himself cast on the open sea without anything to shelter him:

> Nominalism is an extremely disturbing system for man's relationship to the world—to be sure, with the intention of making sure that he cannot find his salvation in the world, of pushing him to despair of his possibilities herebelow, and thus to surrender completely to the act of faith, which he, however, does not have the right to

28 *Ibid.*, p. 227.

perform by his own resources. After the classical philosophy of the Greeks, the possibility of *ataraxia* still remained; after the theological absolutism of the end of the Middle Ages, self-affirmation became the consequence of the entire philosophical system.[29]

Thus it was *rabies theologica* (i.e., theological excess) which entailed, indirectly, theology's own short-circuiting:

The fact of carrying theology to its extreme claim against reason had for its unintended result reducing to a minimum theology's participation in the explanation of the world. Thus the ground was prepared for the competence of reason as the instrument of a new scientificity that was about to liberate itself from tradition.[30]

Or again:

The theological function assigned to a step taken by thought, and which is once again a denial of the confidence that man has vis-à-vis the world, is but the preparation of its contrary human function. To the extent that it vindicates the consciousness of finitude as definitive, theology destroys itself. By underlining the absence of consideration and restraint on the part of the Power opposite man, it implies that in the field of history the neutrality of theoretical progress and indifference towards technological realization cannot exist. By vindicating purported limits and impossibilities, it fatally exposes itself, as it had already done, and would do so again with the proofs for God's existence and theodicy.[31]

---

29 *Ibid.*, p. 167.
30 *Ibid.*, p. 405.
31 *Ibid.*, p. 434.

The transition to the study and conquest of the world is the result of an internal dialectic of Christianity, whose logic destroys its very own existential conditions:

> A religion that, beyond the hope of salvation and confidence in justification, has, according to its own ambition, historically become an exclusive system of explaining the world, and which could deduce, beginning from the fundamental idea of Creation and the idea that man was made in the image of God, the congruence of his faculty of knowing to Nature, but which ended in the medieval version of its concern to preserve the infinite power and absolute liberty of God by destroying the conditions it previously posed to establish man's relationship to the world, such a religion remains ineluctably indebted to man for its good, by the fact of this contradictory reversal of its presuppositions. By this anticipation of the principal thesis of the second part, I do not wish to describe Christianity's entire history, but its crisis at the end of the Middle Ages, that is to say, the conditions for the formation of modern rationality.[32]

In reading this one thinks of Nietzsche, who saw in the love of truth at all costs (*Redlichkeit*), issued from Christianity, the principle of the self-destruction of the latter.[33] With this difference, that the Nietzschean "dialectic" is here transposed into an historical key and limited to the medieval form of Christianity.

Here too, I have to ask: Do the historians of medieval philosophy still speak of such a thing as "nominalism"? Does this category have any value? Is it certain that the purported "nominalism" provoked a *Weltangst*, an anxiety before the omnipotence of an unpredictable God comparable to that experienced by ancient man before the infinity of the heavens?[34]

32 *Ibid.*, p. 128.
33 F. Nietzsche, *Genealogy of Morals*, III, # 27.
34 H. Blumenberg, *LN*, p. 188,

Blumenberg's Middle Ages

The view of the Middles Ages presupposed by Blumenberg does not go without raising certain questions.

On one hand, he sees the Middle Ages as a bloc, and as an historical subject. For example, one reads sentences like: "The Middle Ages, in the fullness of the forms in which it manifests itself, would not have been thinkable without this fundamental axiom."[35] He, moreover, is perfectly aware of the problem of so proceeding, as he indicates in a parenthetical remark: "the Middle Ages, *if one can thus hypostasize.*" Beyond that, somewhere he writes that it is a matter of "a conflict that, in the Middle Ages, was never acknowledged, perhaps *never even felt.*"[36] How can what is never felt produce effects? Supposing that this is the case, the effort to gain access to it, and even to make it the secret engine of an historically assignable attitude, should be conducted with great care, taking a thousand precautions.

In addition, the history Blumenberg recounts develops along only one *phylum* as it were: it is exclusively European and "Christian." It would be interesting to attempt the comparison with Islam. Blumenberg's argument would have lost nothing, but would have gained in perspective. Let me make three points:

(1) Blumenberg, as we saw, attributed great importance to the expectation of the impending end of time in Jesus's preaching and in primitive Christianity. Now, Mohammed's preaching itself began with an apocalyptic message and the announcement of a near judgment. An historian, the Frenchman Paul Casanova (1861–1926), a professor at the Collège de France who today is too often forgotten, put this aspect of things at the center of his interpretation of the beginnings of Islam.[37]

But the problem of "the delay of the parousia" was not raised

---

35 *Ibid.,* p. 403; see also pp. 87 and 393.
36 *Ibid.,* p. 415, then p. 201.
37 P. Casanova, *Mohammed et la fin du monde. Étude critique sur l'islam primitive*, Paris, Geuthner, 1911–1924, 3 vol.

in Islam. One knows the famous phrase of Alfred Loisy: "One expected the Kingdom of God, it was the Church that came." Above all, one knows its most widespread interpretation, which would see in it the acknowledgement of a betrayal, but which is a total misinterpretation of what Loisy meant.[38] In any case, in Islam it was indeed a reign of God that came. In place of the Church, which leaves the kingdom of God outside of it by placing it at the end of times, one had the Muslim city, which incorporates the reign of God in a political order. "Salvation" becomes "peace" (*salām*), the latter being taken in the sense of the *pax romana*. This "peace" is the freedom for the authentic worship of the sole God to be exercised in all security under the protection of a Muslim regime.

The "gnostic" aspects of the religion consequently end, after many vicissitudes, by assuming a more tranquil aspect, to the point where they enter into large swaths of mysticism. The term *'irfān* which denotes this tendency reproduces the Greek word *gnōsis*. In it one encounters, like the Gnosticism of the second century A. D., a radical negation of the world. But its accent is different. The original gnosis affirmed the existence of the world; it even acknowledged its weighty presence. In contrast, though, it denied its value. On the other hand, Islamic "Gnosticism" affirms the value of a beautiful world, which allows its Creator to be manifest. However, it denies that it has a real existence, God being the sole True existent, and it sees in the world only a symbol.

(2) With the Kalām, and above all in the school that took the lead ever since the ninth century until our days (or almost), that is, the school of al-Aš'ari,[39] Islam developed a "theological absolutism" which the most extreme nominalism would have nothing

---

38 See J.-M. Salamito, *Les Chevaliers de l'apocalypse. Réponse à MM. Mordillat et Prieur*, Paris, Lethielleux et Desclée de Brouwer, 2009, chap. V: "Loisy sans Loisy," pp. 47–61.
39 See H. A. Wolfson, *The Philosophy of the Kalām*, Harvard University Press, 1976, and D. Gimaret, *La Doctrine d'Al-Ash'arî*, Cerf, Paris, 1990.

to envy. It is not out of the question, in fact, that the latter may have borrowed some of its ideas from the Kalām, by the intermediary of al-Ghazālî's critique of the notion of causality.[40] Now, Islam does not seem to have felt the anxiety that Blumenberg perceives at the end of the Western Middle Ages, and only in the West. It however does know anxiety before the omnipotence of an unpredictable God when it comes to his decision to save or damn.[41] But there was not a countermovement of reaction which led to a "Modernity."

In Judaism, the battle against the Kalām and in favor of the science of nature was won thanks to Maimonides, at least in certain milieux and for a certain time (before the invasion by the Kabbalah). In Islam the only equivalent was Averroes, who hardly had any posterity, if it wasn't among the Jews, then, partly by their intermediary, the Christians.

(3) The explicit condemnation of intellectual curiosity is characteristic of Christianity, and one must ask why.[42] Islam hardly knows it, to the point that the word is rather difficult to render in Arabic. As for the thing itself, the saying of Ibn Khaldûn is well known: "The questions <pertaining> to the natural sciences have no importance for our religion (*dīn*) and our daily lives (*ma'āš*), so much so that we should leave them to the side."[43] But the Tunisian historian remains an exception. The

40 The question remains disputed; see W. J. Courtenay, "The Critique of Natural Causality in the Mutakallimum and Nominalism," *Harvard Theological Review*, v. 66, 1973, pp. 77–94.

41 See T. Nagel, *Die Festung des Glaubens ...* , *op. cit.*, pp. 99 and 110.

42 See F. Rosenthal, *Knowledge Triumphant. The Concept of Knowledge in Medieval Islam*, Leyde, Brill, 1970; see also my sketch: "L'idée de curiosité dans le judaïsme et l'islam prémodernes. Pour ouvrir un dossier," in G. Freudenthal, J.-P. Rothschild and G. Dahan (ed.), *Torah et Science. Perspectives historiques et théoriques. Études offertes à C. Touati*, Paris and Louvain, Peeters, 2001, pp. 131–46.

43 Ibn Khaldûn, *Muqaddima*, VI, "Réfutation de la philosophie," ed. E. Quatremère, Paris, Duprat, 1858, t. III, p. 214, 15–17; trans. A. Cheddadi, Paris, Gallimard, "Bibliothèque de la Pléiade," 2002, p. 1038.

praise of inquiry is rather the rule. It is found among heterodox personalities, such as Râzî, who, if he belongs to Muslim civilization, can hardly pass for a Muslim because he denies prophecy. His positive view of the effort to know and his acceptance of the relativity of all knowledge, which implies the idea of progress, are rare in Muslim lands.[44] And the Sincere Brethren, of whom I spoke above and who are close to Ismailism, give as an argument in favor of Creation something that resembles the Kantian notion of an "interest of reason": according to them, to deny Creation leads one to renounce the search for knowledge.[45]

However, even the thinkers most concerned to affirm their orthodoxy sought various means to base the search for knowledge on the authority of the Holy Book, or the sayings of the Prophet. Pertaining to this strategy, for example, is the fruitful misinterpretation of the famous *hadith*: "Seek knowledge, even if in China" (*utlubû 'l-'ilm law fî sîn*). The original meaning of it was: "Don't hesitate to take long voyages to receive from the very mouths of the companions of the Prophet or those who knew him, and who are dispersed to the very ends of the Muslim world, the traditions concerning the facts and deeds of the Prophet."[46] It was interpreted, and is still interpreted today by modernizing spirits, as praise of natural science.

The Koran does contain many invitations to consider nature. But what these marvels ought to reveal is above all the power that God has to bring novelty into the world (and thus to raise the dead, in order to subject them to judgment), and less the wisdom that is manifest in the regularity of phenomena. Faithful or unfaithful to the original meaning of the Koran, Averroes

---

44 See the discussion between the two Râzî in *Opera philosophica*, ed. P. Kraus, Cairo, 1939, p. 302 ff. Râzî is treated as a *fudûlî* ("who goes too far, by dealing with things that don't pertain to him") by Avicenna (*ibid.*, p. 290).

45 *Épitres*, III, 8 [39], *op. cit.*, t. III, p. 340.

46 See I. Goldziher, *Études sur la tradition islamique*, trans. L. Bercher, Paris, A. Maisonneuve, 1952, p. 219.

recommends the consideration (i`tibār) of the created world as a path to the knowledge of the Creator.[47] In Judaism, Gersonides, who was himself a practicing astronomer, makes knowledge of the physical universe the cause of final beatitude: the intensity of "salvation" is a function of the quantity of actualized concepts.[48]

Curiosity

Blumenberg's book implies a reflection on the role of Christianity in the intellectual history of the West, which would be unthinkable without it.[49] For my part, I would have placed certain emphases differently. Let's begin with a detail: Did the idea of infinite progress appear for the first time in Pascal?[50] Now Blumenberg, one of whose merits is precisely to have reintegrated the Fathers of the Church into the history of thought, obviously is not ignorant that the idea is found in Gregory of Nyssa.[51] He formulated it in his theory of eternal beatitude, which is conceived not as fixity in contemplation, but as a constant deepening in the knowledge of the infinite God, as the "eternal furious ascent towards the Absolute," as Leon Bloy will say later.[52]

To be sure, the context is different, but this difference is precisely the interesting point, because it obliges us to reconsider the

47 See W. Z. Harvey, "Averroès et Maïmonide sur le devoir philosophique de contempler (i`tibār)" [Hebrew], Tarbiz, v. 58, n. 1 (1988), pp. 75–83.
48 See G. Freudenthal, "Sauver son âme ou sauver les phénomènes: sotériologie, épistémologie et astronomie chez Gersonide," in G. Freudenthal (ed.), Studies in Gersonides. A Fourteenth-Century Jewish Philosopher-Scientist, Leyden and New York, Brill, 1992, pp. 317–52.
49 H. Blumenberg, LN, p. 39 (and see p. 128).
50 H. Blumenberg, LN, p. 94.
51 See the texts cited in H. U. von Balthasar, Présence et Pensée. Essai sur la philosophie religieuse de Grégoire de Nysse, Paris, Beauchesne, 1988 (2nd ed.), pp. 123–32.
52 L. Bloy, Le Désespéré, II, chap. XXXVII.

reasons for the Christian critique of curiosity.[53] Augustine is one of the principal witnesses here. However, it was he who wrote, apropos to God: "He is infinite so that, once we have found him, we will seek him <even more>" (*ut inventus quaeratur, immensus est*).[54]

One thus sees the ultimate reason for the critique of curiosity, which Blumenberg elsewhere glimpses in connection with Thomas Aquinas[55]: *Curiositas* for the creature is, paradoxically, a weakness in the desire to know, a lack of ambition, because God is the sole infinite field for human desire. If the Fathers of the Church in their polemics against Gnosticism critiqued the insatiable desire to search or inquire,[56] it is because this desire is mistaken not about its object, but its *field*: the infinite of the created must cede to the "infinitely infinite" of God. Thus, what can appear to be a limitation of curiosity is in fact a way of liberating it, by assigning to God the sole field within which it can give itself free rein, and vis-à-vis which the created is insufficient and hence unsatisfying.

Therefore the endorsements of inquiry into nature such as those that I cited above from Muslim or Jewish thinkers are rare among Christian authors. However, contrary to what one would have expected, it was in a Christian milieu that modern natural science developed. Blumenberg well explains why. A comparative perspective would only have enriched his views.

Providence

In the following passage, Blumenberg indicates what the fundamental limitation of the medieval vision of things was that made the transition to Modern Times necessary:

53 See G. Bös, *Curiositas. Die Rezeption eines antiken Begriffes durch christliche Autoren bis Thomas von Aquin*, Paderborn, Schöningh, 1995.
54 St. Augustine, *Commentaire de l'Évangile de Jean*, 63, 1, ed. R. Willems (CCSL XXXVI), p. 485.
55 H. Blumenberg, *LN*, p. 387.
56 *Ibid.*, p. 416.

The Middle Ages came to an end when they could no longer make man believe, at the core of his spiritual system, that creation was providential, and when by that fact they imposed upon him the burden of self-affirmation. "Self-affirmation" therefore does not mean here simply the biological and economic preservation of the human animal by the means that his nature provides. It signifies an existential program under which man, in a given historical situation, places his existence, and which he inscribes as he wishes to perceive it in the midst of the reality that surrounds him, and how he wants to exploit its possibilities. In the comprehension of the world, and the implied expectations, valuations and interpretations, a fundamental metamorphosis takes place which is not merely the addition of the facts of experience, but a collection of assumptions that in their turn determine the horizon of possible experiences and their interpretation, and contain the prevenient givens of what the world means for man.[57]

The idea of Providence is thus conceived as the cornerstone of the medieval enterprise. As a result, its collapse must entail the fall of the entire edifice. If it is true that the failure of Providence makes the auto-affirmation of man inevitable, one clearly sees what this idea implies, to wit: that the affirmation (*Behauptung*) of man was not till then (yet) a *self*-affirmation, that it was not the doing of man himself, but of authorities external to him. These authorities were designated by the words "nature" and "God" (or the two notions coming together, for example, in the divinized nature of the Stoics).

Here one has to ask Blumenberg if the notion of Providence can be reduced to the *pronoia* of the pagans, from Herodotus to the aforementioned Stoics. To be sure, the *concept* of Providence had to wait for the Greeks. But what to make of the biblical ana-

57 *Ibid.*, p. 151.

logues and approaches to the idea? The Old Testament sees it at work in nature (*Ps.* 104) and in the course of events, for example, in the history of Joseph (*Genesis*, 45, 5b.7–8a; 50, 20). And the New Testament speaks of the divine design of the adoption of all of humanity recapitulated in Christ (*Eph.* 1, 10).

The notion of *Selbstbehauptung*, which Blumenberg puts at the center of the first part of his book, is not easy to translate into English, and "self-affirmation," with which I have had to be content, is only used for lack of a better word. In order to have an adequate one, one would have to bring to light all the resonances of the metaphor of "head" (*Haupt*), from "raise one's head" to "totally in one's head," while passing by everything that Derrida's virtuosity could tease out from the cognates of the Latin *caput* (head): cap, chef, capital, etc.[58]

Still, it is essentially a matter of a way of determining oneself, precisely by oneself. But not necessarily in a positive way and, hence, an affirmation. Nothing prohibits a self-determination from taking on the traits of self-negation. Thus, one must add to the idea of self-affirmation an element that keeps it from turning into suicide, which guarantees—if I can be permitted an etymological play on words—that *Selbstbehauptung* is a "recapitulation" (*anakephalaiōsis*) in the creative Word.

What Middle Ages do we want?

We can now ask if Modern Times have truly done better than the Middle Ages. How can you ask that?! some will exclaim. You want "a new Middle Ages"?! If that were the case, I would not be the first to do so. I have already mentioned Berdyaev's book. He did not remain without imitators.[59] To be sure, many mediocrities today raise the specter of the Middle Ages as a scare tactic, in order to reassure, and to sell their books to, a contemporary audience.

58 J. Derrida, *L'Autre Cap*, Paris, Minuit, 1991
59 See W. Welsh, *Unsere postmoderne Moderne*, Berlin, Akademie Verlag, 1997 (5th ed.), pp. 57–59.

They presume that there is a widespread image of the Middle Ages as the Dark Ages. Some parallel the situation of Western Europe after the collapse of the Roman Empire with what happened once the Soviet Empire collapsed, or risks happening if the American one does.[60] Rarer, but no less interesting, are those who see in present developments quite positive parallels with what was possible in the medieval period.[61]

According to my lights, however, the question is not whether we want the Middle Ages to return. We do not need to wish for this return. It is inevitable.

Therefore I am going to let small minds feign fear, trot out the pejorative "reactionary!", and pretend that they are "brave resisters."

The real question is to know *what sort of Middle Ages* we would wish, or rather: what sort we *ought* to desire to return. To be precise, I am not speaking of economic or medical arrangements or practices: the progress achieved by Modern Times is spectacular (albeit inaugurated by great technical inventions of the Middle Ages). Nor am I speaking about political life: the medieval period was the contrary of a time of order and harmony, but rather a time of great confusion. Pierre Manent was quite correct to recall this recently.[62]

Here, I am placing myself entirely on the plane of thought, or, if you prefer, of vision of the world. For Blumenberg, the Middle Ages did not know how to propose a truly credible alternative to Gnosticism. But have Modern Times succeeded? In this connection it is quite interesting to note that it was at that very moment that a rigorous formulation was given at the conceptual level, especially by Schopenhauer, of what remained at the level of intuitions, im-

60 A. Minc, *Le Nouveau Moyen Âge*, Paris, Gallimard, 1993.

61 Thus U. Eco, "Verso un nuovo Medioevo" [1972], *Dalla periferia dell'Impero. Cronache da un nuovo Medioevo*, Milan, Bompiani, 1977, pp. 189–211.

62 P. Manent, *Le Regard politique*, Paris, Flammarion, 2010, pp. 160–63.

ages or myths among the Gnostics. Moreover, this Gnostic vision of things receives, as I recalled above,[63] powerful support from modern science. We therefore need to revise our judgment concerning the medieval vision of the world and see in its conception of creation and Providence the indispensable condition of the continuation of the human adventure.

Indeed, the Middle Ages—whatever may be the severity of the judgment that one would like to make in their regard—at least had the merit of having a posterity by (to change the metaphor) uncorking Modernity. In contrast, one can ask if over the long term the latter is pregnant with anything other than unvarnished nihilism. Unless, that is, it ends in something worse than the most caricatural view of the Middle Ages, whose darkness would make any purported medieval darkness appear to be blinding light. Why? This would no longer be a darkness *before* Enlightenment, but an obscurantism that would have taken the measure of what enlightenment could be and rejected it *en pleine connaissance de cause.*

I am a little ashamed to have to state the obvious, but for me it is *not* a matter of rejecting all that has occurred since the end of the medieval period. It is obvious that one cannot do away with the time that has elapsed or erase the memory of the rich experience that Modernity has brought—even if the second would in some sense be easier than the first, which is purely and simply impossible. In any event, it is a gross *non sequitur* to conclude from the irreversibility of time to that of its contents. A return is always possible, even if it is not desirable except in certain cases. It can happen, though, that a return of this sort is the indispensable condition for progress.

And in particular, in daily life, for a pedestrian as for a driver, to back up is the most reasonable course of action when one finds oneself in a blind alley. To extricate oneself from it becomes the indispensable condition allowing one to return to the turn one missed, and thus to begin anew.

---

63 See *supra*, p. 31.

Chapter VIII
Who Makes Man?

The Middle Ages allowed an affirmation of man because it believed that his very humanity depended on a principle distinct from him, which gave him being. It conceived man as a creature of God, often represented as acting through the intermediary of nature. For us, the question of man's origin has to be raised anew. One has to ask again: What made or makes man? Who or what deserves to be called his creator?

In this way, once again the question of legitimacy comes close to its original connotations having to do with the order of filiation. If the line has no ancestor, the question loses its point and becomes null. Man becomes a sort of bastard who has no progenitor, a natural child who is so natural that he would not even be the descendant of anyone.

Self-creation?

A shortcut would be to say that man is his own creator. Then the question would not have to be raised. Formulations suggesting the idea are found in German idealism, where they nonetheless have an acceptable meaning, for example in Schelling: "The essence of man is his action."[1] Then, however, they entered and took over the rhetoric of existentialism, first of all with Sartre, but even more his

---

1   See F. W. Schelling, *Philosophische Untersuchungen über das Wesen der menschlichen Freiheit und die damit zusammenhängenden Gegenstände* [1809], in *Sämtliche Werke*, Darmstadt, Wissenschaftliche Buchgesellschaft, 1976, t. VII, p. 385.

epigones up to our day. Repeated as mantras are sentences like the following: "Man is nothing but his own project," and even more radically: "I am my project."[2] That can be said, because language is an obedient child. But can it be *thought*?

The sentences can represent a hyperbolic way of expressing a platitude: we are free, and our past does not predetermine the way in which we ought decide our future, since "our history is not our code." In another, more positive and profound way, Hannah Arendt proposed the concept of "natality": the birth of every human being is a new beginning.[3] To spoil a lovely idea like that with pretentious formulas like the ones I cited is hardly more than bad rhetoric.

But it is also bad logic. In strict terms, the sentence is untenable and fails upon inspection. How can one give any meaning to the possessive adjective "my"? How can a project be mine if the "I" is constructed by the project? We find the same circular absurdity in the sentence of the young Marx, who explained that man is rendered man by *human* work.[4]

The trouble is that, as always, violated logic takes its revenge. It does so by giving birth to another phrase, this one unacknowledged, which is the truth of the absurd one that masks it. "I am *a* project." The question then immediately becomes: of whom or what is man in general, and I in particular, the project? "Nature"? If one tries to clarify what hides behind that august term, one has to acknowledge an impersonal fate. Or refusing that, one that leads to the suppression of the self. In the first case, freedom would turn against itself; in the second, it reduces to the suppression of the subject that bears it. Self-creation turns into the destruction of the self by the self.

2   J.-P. Sartre, *L'existentialisme est un humanisme*, Paris, Nagel, 1946, p. 55; see also pp. 23 & 69–70; and *Cahiers pour une morale*, Paris, Gallimard, 1983, p. 267.

3   H. Arendt, *The Human Condition*, The University of Chicago Press, 1963, p. 9 ff.

4   K. Marx, *Manuscrits de 1844*, III, in K. Marx and F. Engels, *Werke*, Ergänzungsband, Berlin, Dietz, 1968, p. 98.

Suicide

Is nature capable of producing a species that desires its own destruction? Or in any case can envisage it? The capacity to commit suicide is specific to man, and does not seem to have any real parallel among other animals.[5] For example, we know now that the collective drowning of lemmings was only one of a number of cinematographic fictions of Walt Disney.

Some have sought for prefigurations of suicide in the more elementary levels of life. Thus, some have wanted to explain certain phenomena connected with maturation in plants by a kind of self-pruning.[6] However, what since 1972 has been called "apoptosis," i.e., the disappearance of cells that are no longer useful to the organ and act as if they "felt" they were superfluous and thus ceased to reproduce, is not really comparable.[7]

The facts as biology has established them are these: a whole does away with a part that would inhibit its subsequent development. Everything thus occurs as if the part "sacrificed" itself for the whole. This, however, is only rarely the case with an individual of the human species, out of *devotio* for the collectivity. It would be even less plausible in the case of a universal suicide, because one would have to ask: for whose (or what's) sake would the species commit suicide?

In any case, the mere fact that nature produces a species that can envisage its own destruction shows that it is not so easy to see

5   See H. Bergson, *Les Deux Sources de la morale et de la religion*, chap. II, Paris, Alcan, 1932, p. 135.

6   The notion was probably introduced by J. H. Schaffner and F. Tyler, "Notes on the Self-Pruning of Trees," *The Ohio Naturalist*, v. 1, n. 3 (January 1901), pp. 29–32. https://kb.osu.edu/dspace/bitstream/handle/1811/1189/V01N03_029.pdf;jsessionid=248224DDE2044F8E62 0669A3B1EEE55B?sequence=1.

7   See J. F. R. Kerr, A. H. Willie and A. R. Currie, "Apoptosis: A Basic Biological Phenomenon with Wide-Ranging Implications in Tissue Kinetics," *British Journal of Cancer*, v. 26, n. 4 (August 1972), pp. 239–57. http://www.nature.com/bjc/journal/v26/n4/pdf/bjc197233a.pdf.

this species as the pure product of nature. If natural selection decides everything and has only allowed characteristics that are useful to the survival of the species, one can hardly see how the awareness of finitude as such ("one day, I must die") could be useful to it. To assure its permanence, it would suffice to have an instinctive fear of pain, accompanied by strategies that would allow it to avoid it. This has already been pointed out by Max Scheler.[8] Even more mysterious is the desire to anticipate death by killing oneself.

Sartre himself does not take very seriously his own formulation and recalls the obvious: man "did not create himself."[9] To unpack the thought: on one hand, there exists a living thing that is so made that it can engage in projects whose content is not dictated in advance by anything other than itself; on the other hand, this living thing is itself the product of something else.

Now, once one has admitted that man did not make himself, one can put forth certain fundamental alternatives: Is he the work of an impersonal power, or of a "person," more precisely: a "superperson"? Was everything done by chance, i.e., in virtue of the interplay of factors whose relationships are regulated by necessary natural laws? Or can one find traces of an intention? In which case, is it benevolent?

Evolution?

The man in the street has the habit of responding to the question, what produced the human species to which you belong?, with the answer he has heard a thousand times: "Evolution!" The capital letter that he gives the word, like one does with a proper name, helps him see it as a conscious agent, even though the concept denies any intentional character to the process.

We should first note that this is merely a quick way of referring to something, one that only satisfies popularizers. It is no more rigorous to say "Evolution has produced man" than to say "History

8   M. Scheler, *Schriften zur Anthropologie, op. cit.*, p. 81.
9   J.-P. Sartre, *L'existentialisme est un humanisme, op. cit.*, p. 37.

produced Napoleon." In the two cases there is an effort to summarize a complex whole with many interacting factors.

In its dominant version, formulated by Darwin, evolution is a matter of the survival of the fittest in the struggle for life, which takes place in a competition for scarce resources.[10] The whole edifice is placed on the foundation of a vital force supposed to seek to increase, or at least maintain itself, at whatever cost. This, as one can see, cannot be conceptualized without something like a metaphysics of life.

Bergson's observations on this seem to be entirely relevant. He presents them in a work in which he reflects on the evolutionary idea and notes the inadequacy of a purely mechanical explanation: "Adaptation explains the twists-and-turns of the evolutionary movement, but not its general directions, much less the movement itself."[11] Or, a few years later: "This necessity seems to explain the way life stops at such-and-such determinate forms, but not the movement which carries the organization higher and higher."[12]

If one decides to ignore these objections, one will say that man is only the product of chance, but this word too will have to be seen as merely a convenient shorthand, since chance is not a cause properly speaking, but the encounter of a series of independent causes. In this way it's the sobriquet, not of Providence, but of necessary natural laws.

Here the trouble is that supposing that this is the case, man would have no reason to continue to proceed in the direction of the causes that have led to him, and to prolong them. Why should he transform them into *reasons* to continue on the same path? Why should he be obliged to continue to do consciously and freely what made him unconsciously and unfreely? Man would have no reason

10 C. Darwin, *The Origin of Species by Means of Natural Selection or the Preservation of Favored Races in the Struggle for Life* [1859], New York, The Modern Library, s.d.
11 H. Bergson, *L'Évolution créatrice*, chap. II, Paris, Alcan, 1907, p. 103.
12 H. Bergson, "La Conscience et la Vie" [1911], *L'Énergie spirituelle*, Paris, Alcan, 1919, p. 18.

to pursue the adventure of history. Perhaps he would even have reasons—and excellent ones—to bring it to an end.

Gaia?

Something superior to the human, a divinity therefore, would be at the origin of our existence? But of what sort?

One knows Nietzsche's *cri de coeur*: "What, two thousand years already and not a single new god!"[13] It would be difficult to be more thoroughly mistaken. In truth, new gods have not been lacking; quite the contrary, they proliferated. The most attractive ones were those that presented themselves explicitly as such. Thus, those new religions that appeared in the midst of the nineteenth century, and of which Nietzsche could have heard: the Mormons, the Bahai's, without counting the ephemeral civic cults that were patched together at the time of the French Revolution.

Other gods avoid presenting themselves as such. And truth be told, they are not always very friendly; some are even frankly perverse. Thus, this recurring nightmare, one I have already invoked: artificial intelligence, inanimate, merely mineral, in relationship to which man (and even all of life) would only be a provisional scaffolding that can be rejected once it has done its work.[14] Or the Earth, in whose name one envisages getting rid of man in order to restore its pristine purity. As we saw earlier, certain aspects of the ecological movement are in this way a modern resurgence of the religion of nature.[15]

The modern version of the idea of the divinity of the Earth is as old as Auguste Comte. At the end of his life, the father of positivism proposed completing the religion of Humanity, or the Great-Being situated within the universe or "Great Milieu," with "a just adoration of the Earth, held up as the Great Fetish, seat and station

13 F. Nietzsche, *L'Antéchrist*, # 19, in KSA, t. VI, p. 185.
14 See supra, pp. 33–34.
15 See J. Radkau, *Natur und Macht. Eine Weltgeschichte der Umwelt*, Munich, Beck, 2000, pp. 254–60.

of the Great-Being."[16] At the same period, the physiologist and psychologist Gustav Theodor Fechner saw in the Earth a living being.[17] Certain contemporary thinkers claim to see in the Earth, or the biosphere, a whole which they call Gaia. This theory with scientific aspirations initially aimed to express the way in which each living thing interacts on all. But the name was taken up and transposed into a religious register by the New Age movement.

For some of its representatives, man would represent a mortal danger to the biosphere by his mere existence and the uncontrollable inclination he has to claim everything for himself. It therefore is necessary to show him the exit door, if one wants to preserve life on the earth.

However, there is a difficulty: If the globe created a being that threatens its existence, the higher spheres committed a blunder. The divinity assumed to be superior to man is dumb. In this way, one has to sacrifice the greater to save the lesser.

The dark alternative posed by A. E. Housman, in a poem where a person curses "whatever brute or blackguard made the world," is well known.[18] In the hypothesis I just examined, that of a divine and creative Earth, the issue is decided in terms of the first possibility: what made man is a stupid brute.

But the second remains.

Blackguard?

The widespread expression, "the good Lord," is far from always having been as obvious as it is for us. Nietzsche, with his god "beyond good and evil," whom he would prefer to the "moral god,"

---

16 A. Comte, *Synthèse subjective ou Système universel des conceptions propres à l'état normal de l'humanité*, "Introduction," *op. cit.*, p. 14; see also pp. 23, 34, 50, 53–54, and 107.

17 G. T. Fechner, *Zend-Avesta oder über die Dinge des Himmels und des Jenseits. Von Standpunkt der Naturbetrachtung* [1851], chap. V, Leipzig, Voβ, 1922 (5th ed.), t. I, pp. 139–43.

18 A. E. Housman, "The Chestnut Casts His Flambeaux," *Last Poems* [1922].

expressed a wonderful optimism. The idea of the jealousy of gods towards men, from whom they hide the good things of life, is quite ancient, for example, in the myth of Prometheus. Herodotus, alongside a rather rationalistic vision of the world, still says that the divine is envious (*phtoneron*) and ready to create problems (*tarakhodes*).[19]

To create is one thing, to affirm and confirm in existence what one created is another. A creative power who contents itself with producing as sport, in order to enjoy the subsequent destruction of what it produced, this is not an unheard of idea. It is found in the Hindu eighth century among the thinkers of the Vedanta, or in the Persia of the eleventh century with Omar Khayyam and his image of the pieces on the checkerboard that are put in the box after the initial arrangement.[20]

I have already alluded to a god beyond good and evil, the form of the divine that Nietzsche saw emerge after the "molting" by which the divine would have shed his moral epidermis.[21] This zoological image borrowed from snakes should make us cautious about the nature of this god returned to its primitive nakedness . . .

The idea of an incompetent or even perverse, frankly evil, demiurge is also found in Gnosticism. This evil god of Gnosticism (or of Manicheanism) is in a way more plausible than the God of the Bible, if one seeks an easy explanation for the presence of evil in the world. That there is a principle of good and, alongside it, a principle of evil—here is an intellectually inexpensive answer. Thus there is nothing surprising in the fact that this explanation constantly tempted the West, from Augustine to André Breton, while passing through Voltaire's *Candide*, in which one of the rare sympathetic characters is Martin, a Manichean.

Epicurus believed he caught those who thought that the gods

---

19 Herodotus, I, 32, 1; III, 40, 2.
20 Badarayana, *Brahma Sutra*, II, 1, # 33 (167); Omar Khayyām, *Rubā'iyāt*, n. 103 in the translation of Franz Toussaint.
21 F. Nietzsche, fragment [3], 432, "Summer-Autumn 1882," in *KSA*, t. X, p. 105.

concerned themselves with worldly affairs in the horns of a dilemma: Since there is evil in the world, either the gods cannot do anything to eradicate it, or they don't want to: they are either weak or wicked. Boethius responded with another alternative: "If there is a god, where do evil things come from?; but where do the good things come from, if there isn't?" (*Si quidem deus [. . .] est, unde mala? Bona vero unde, si non est?*).[22] Boethius quotes this line, but its source is unknown. That does not really matter, since the issue is now raised. Plotinus asked: "Where do evil things come from?" (*pothen ta kaka*) and he had devoted an entire treatise to the question.[23] But that there is good doesn't go without saying, and it requires an explanation as much as the presence of evil. And the presence in the world of a being like man, capable of distinguishing good and evil, of being capable of knowing the good and yet still doing evil, is itself an enigma.

The German poet Gottfried Benn, despite being a pessimist (in the emphatic sense) and a nihilist, composed a little poem on the theme. He cites two examples, both very simple but of great significance. A young woman who never gives her name without also saying how it is spelled, so as not to embarrass those who write it; and an adolescent who lives in truly impoverished conditions but who bravely learns her lessons and exhibits the dignity of an aristocratic lady. He ends the poem with these words: "I've often asked myself, without finding an answer, where what is gentle, what is good, comes from. I don't know any more today, but I've gotta go." (*Ich habe mich oft gefragt und keine Antwort gefunden, / woher das Sanfte und das Gute kommt,/ weiß es auch heute nicht und muß nun gehen.*)[24] Gotta go? After the brief visit of a doctor? (Benn was a doctor.) Or more radically, leaving this world?

---

22 Epicurus, in Lactantius, *De ira Dei*, 13, PL, 7, 121a; Boethius, *De consolatione philosophiae*, I, prose 4, *op. cit.*, p. 152.
23 Plotinus, Enneads, I, 8.
24 G. Benn, "Menschen getroffen" [before June 1955], in *Sämtliche Werke*, ed. G. Schuster and I. Benn, Stuttgart, Klett, t. I: *Gedichte 1*, 1986, p. 301.

The God of Genesis

What about the hypothesis of a creator God? A model of this type of god has been in circulation for centuries, the one we find out about at the beginning of the Bible, in the first creation account of *Genesis*. Such a god "redoubles" his creation by affirming that it is good. I need to spend some time on the text that conveys this model. This is even more necessary today as the idea of creation is too often confused with "creationism," which rests on a naïvely literal reading and results in flattening a text containing inexhaustible depths and riches.

I also need to be explicit: in turning to this text, I have no intention of comparing and contrasting it with the vision of things proposed by certain sciences of nature (astrophysics, geology, paleontology, zoology), and in particular their reconstruction of cosmogenesis. In contrast to all that, the biblical narrative furnishes a model of an answer to a question that the sciences do not treat, to wit: the *value* of what exists. The sciences describe reality, but it is not theirs to say if it is good or bad. In its turn, the first creation account provides no explanation of the coming-to-be of things, but it does affirm that everything created is "good."

How to understand this declaration? It is solemnly repeated after each of the five days, and is raised to a higher level after the sixth and last of the days of creation: once finished and taken in by a synoptic view, what is created is said to be "very good" (*Genesis*, I, 31).

Why was this affirmation necessary? To what did it respond? One does not solemnly affirm what is obvious and goes without saying; one recalls what runs the risk of being neglected or forgotten. What temptation does it wish to exorcize? Schopenhauer took this verse of the Bible, which he cites in the Greek of the Septuagint, as the favorite target of his sarcasms and the synthesis of everything he could not accept. To what earlier pessimism, more than two millennia earlier than that of the German philosopher, did *Genesis* seek to oppose?

One has found a possible trace of prebiblical pessimism in a famous Egyptian text, especially since it could have been a remote source of the book of Job, the *Dialogue avec son* ba *de l'homme fatigué de vivre* (the dialogue of the man tired of life with his ba).[25] This, however, is merely the "feeling blue" of a psychological state, and that text does not rise to a condemnation of the world as a whole.

In contrast, certain creation myths made creation a violent act. This is true of Babylonian accounts, with which the Jewish elite was probably in contact when they were held hostage in Babylon. According to the leading cosmology, creation consisted in a murder. It was accomplished by a savior god. The victim was a primitive monster, Tiamat (the Hebrew word *tehom* ["the abyss" covered with "darkness] perhaps retains a trace of it). The savior god, Marduk, would have split the cadaver into two pieces, which made heaven and earth.[26] The world was thus the result of a crime. Hence, it is fundamentally illegitimate.

As for man, according to the Akkadian cosmological epic, *Enuma Elish*, he was created from the blood of a vanquished god. Therefore, he too is the result of an act of violence. Moreover, he is predestined to be the slave of the gods. He is tasked with their work details and thus allows them to lead a joyful life.[27]

This way of seeing things had a long life, even with Christians. Thus certain Fathers of the Church, whose thought continued into the Middle Ages, were very close to the idea according to which the creation of men was only a second-best option. They would hardly be anything more than substitutes, charged with filling the places in the celestial ranks left empty by the desertion of the fallen angels.[28]

---

25 Text in W. Barta, *Das Gespräch eines Mannes mit seinem BA (Papyrus Berlin 3024)*, Berlin, Hessling, 1969.
26 *Enuma Elish*, tablet IV, 136, in J. B. Pritchard, *Ancient Near Eastern Texts Relating to the Old Testament*, Princeton University Press, 1955, p. 67b.
27 *Enuma Elish*, tablet VI, 5–8, *ibid.*, p. 68a.
28 See, for example, St. Augustine, *Cité de Dieu*, XXII, 1, *op. cit.*, t. II, p. 748; Bernard of Clairvaux, *Homélie pour la fête de saint Michel*, I, 4, in *Opera*, Rome, Editions cistercienses, 1968, t. V, pp. 296–97.

Goodness of the world, goodness of God

On the basis of these representations, and perhaps against them, the Bible presupposes that God knows no envy and is pure generosity. In Greece, the idea appeared in Plato and was found throughout the Middle Ages.[29] God knows no envy because he has no need of anything. In any event, everything belongs to him. He is therefore not in competition with his creatures, to whom he can give or refuse to give.

The Hebrew Bible expresses the same idea in its own way: "YHWH is good towards all, his tenderness goes to all his works" (*tōv-YHWH lak-kol we-rahamaw 'al-kol-ma' asaw/khrestos kyrios tois hypomenousi/suavis dominus universis*) (*Ps.* 145, 9).

In the Greek Bible, the idea takes the form of an argument: "If God had hated something, He would not have made it" (*Sirach*, 15, 11b). The most recent version of that idea develops it: "Yes, you love all the beings and have antipathy for nothing that you made [*agapas gar ta onta panta kai ouden bdelussès hôn epoièsas*]; for if you had hated something, you would not have established it. And how would something have subsisted, if you had not willed it? How would something not called by you be preserved?/But you spare all things, because <they> belong to you, Master, friend of life." (*Wisdom*, 11, 24–26).[30]

If the goodness of God extends to all, the created must be considered a whole, unified in an order.

In this way the Bible rejoins an idea dear to the Greeks. At the end of a long process of conceptual clarification, they came to think the world as a totality, a whole, and to express this by the word *kosmos*, "ornament." In the same context, *Genesis* prefers to speak of an "army" (*tsava*) (*Genesis*, 2, 1). The word contains precious meaning. It often is used in the phrase "the heavenly

---

29 Plato, *Phaedrus*, 247a; *Timaeus*, 29b; Jehuda Halevi, *Kuzari*, V, 10, op. cit., pp. 199–200.

30 The text is cited by St. Thomas Aquinas, *Summa theologiae*, I, q. 20, *sed contra*.

host," a banal image for the stars, found in the first two parts of the book of *Isaiah* (34, 4; 40, 26), but already implicit in older texts that imagine them organized to fight on the side of the people of Israel (*Judges*, 5, 20). In the second part of the book of *Isaiah*, "the army of the heavens" is distinguished from "the earth" (45, 12). Here in *Genesis*, in an exceptional way, "army" covers and brings together in one image what otherwise was separated, as it were, *toto coelo*. In this way, here the word *tsava* becomes something of a Hebrew prefiguration, preconceptual, of the idea of "world."

Moreover, one can observe that the distance between image and concept is perhaps less great than one might at first think. In fact, the Greeks elaborated their concepts from words in ordinary use, as did all the languages that in their wake became carriers of philosophy. And the conceptual signification of a word issued from its metaphorical use. Now, the underlying image of the Greek concept of *kosmos* is most likely not foreign to the military domain. The oldest occurrences of the term, in Homer, in fact have it designate the good order of an army ready for battle and mounting an attack without relaxing its discipline (*eu kata kosmon*).[31] The order of the world, in ancient Greece as in ancient Israel, is a battle order.

To what "good"?

The goodness of creation, affirmed after each of the days of creation and recapitulated at the end of the entire work of creation, finds its correspondent in the goodness of its author, the Creator of all. Formulaic lines on the "goodness" (*ki tov*) of God found in many psalms are perhaps the literary source of what is affirmed in the creation narratives.

The superlative *"very* good" which concludes the first *Genesis* account has been interpreted in various ways, all become classic. Thus, some have noted that what was already good when separated

31 Homer, *Iliad*, XI, v. 48ff.

is *a fortiori* so when the parts are harmonized in a whole.[32] Or again, it has been understood as "good as a whole," and a theodicy has been inferred, according to which evil would be necessary for good to be. Augustine ranks the goodness of the creatures according to their various levels. "Good" does not mean the same for every creature.[33] All these ideas are also found in pagan philosophy.

But the Bible adds something: this good must not only be received, but produced in history. This is a direct consequence of the fact that no creature, as such, is bad. The sea monsters hidden in the depths of the sea and who "condense" its dangers are themselves created by God (*Genesis*, 1, 21). The stars are also created by God; they however are also responsible for baleful influences, and can easily be taken for objects of idolatrous worship.

In this way the Bible proceeds to a relocation of the problem of evil. "The pagan notion of a primordial evil inherent in creation is banished. As a result, evil must be apprehended on the moral plane and no longer the mythological."[34] Evil ceases to appear as an inevitable necessity. It is henceforth an adversary to combat. A history thus opens, open in what concerns its eventual results, although determined in what concerns the task to perform.

In this way, and to cite one of the most profound commentators on the passage: "The world is "good" not in the sense of a quality that one can establish and observe, but rather in a functional sense: "good for." The world that God created good and found good is the one in which a history that fulfills the meaning of creation can begin and arrive at a good end."[35]

---

32 See, for example, St. Augustine, *De Genesi ad litteram*, III, 24 & 37, ed. J. Zycha, Prague et al., Tempsky (CSEL, 28-1), 1894, p. 92; *De Genesi contra Manichaeos*, I, xxi, 32; PL, 34, 188; Gersonides, *Peyrushey ha-Torah*, ed. Y. L. Levi, Jerusalem, Mosad Rav Kook, 1992, p. 47.

33 St. Augustine, *De diversis quaestionibus* 83, LI, 2, ed. A. Mutzenbecher (CCSL 44), Turnhout, Brepols, 1975, pp. 79–80.

34 N. M. Sarna, *Genesis (JPS Torah Commentary)*, Philadelphia *et al.*, Jewish Publications Society, 1989, p. 7.

35 C. Westermann, *Genesis*, 1, "Teilband, Genesis 1–11," Neukirchen-Vluyn, Neukirchener Verlag, 1974, p. 229.

In the biblical narrative, one is struck by the enumeration of created things, with each being declared "good" at the end of day it came into being (*Genesis* 1, 4. 10. 12. 18. 21. 25). These affirmations are comparable to a check-list that airplane pilots follow before take-off. They verify that all the systems needed for a smooth flight are operational. There is nothing theoretical in this, everything is ordered to action. This is not intended as praise for the different parts that compose the mechanism of the plane, but to assure that it can take off safely.

Creation is "good" in this sense, that it is capable of harboring a freedom, one that creates history. Thus, its "goodness" is not a perfection that would render human action impossible or superfluous. On the contrary, it is what makes action possible and meaningful.

In the image of God

That creation in its entirety is the object of divine approbation is not obvious. That all men are embraced in this approval is even more difficult to admit. It would be easier to imagine that God loves certain men and hates others. This view is found about everywhere. At the margins of the biblical view of the world it is attested to among the sectarians of Qumran and later in the Koran.[36]

By this token, the risk is great to imagine that God is "with us," that He loves those whom we love and hates those whom we hate, and that we therefore can enlist him in our battles. It would be pointless to list all the cases in which humans have succumbed to this temptation, including those who claim the Bible as their sacred Book.

The Greeks too thought the gods were friends of man as such. Thus, Xenophon has Aristodemus, responding to Socrates' questions, say that the advantages showered upon man "have

---

36 *Règle de la communauté* (Qumran, III, 25), in *Die Texte aus Qumran*, ed. E. Lohse, Munich, Kösel, 1964, p. 12; *Koran*, 40, 10.

the appearance of the devices [*tekhnèma*] of a skilled craftsman and friend of life [*philozoos*]."[37] Hellenized Jews could thus draw the same teaching from the two sources of their culture. Philo of Alexandria several times used similar expressions: God displayed friendship with men (*philanthropia*); He loves life (*philozoos*) and man in particular (*philanthropos*); and he refers to Plato's *Timaeus*.[38] The Russian philosopher Leon Chestov distinguishes, in order to oppose them, two conceptions of the world and man's presence on earth, thus ending with a decisive alternative: either man is created in God's image, or he represents "an impious audacity."(нечестивое дерзновение).[39] With the first he obviously alludes to the sentence in the Bible where God created man in His image and as His likeness (*Genesis*, 1, 26). This idea has been commented upon extensively, and it has even been illustrated by the arts. It is what gave birth to a magnificent sculpture in the cathedral of Chartres, which represents the creation of Adam. The features of the newly created man reproduce exactly those of the Creator who is found just behind him, and who is represented according to the traditional canons that regulate the depiction of Christ.

However, "to be created in the image of God" is an expression whose meaning must vary depending upon the type of God one has in mind.

The imitation of the invisible

The God of the Bible is invisible. The "no one has ever seen God" of the New Testament (*John*, 1, 18) sums up a constant of the Old Testament. Moreover, the biblical God forbids that one attempt to

37 Xenophon, *Memorabilia*, I, 4. 7.
38 Philo, Chérubins, 99, ed. J. Gorez, Paris, Cerf, 1963, p. 66; *De specialibus legibus*, III, 36, ed. A. Mosès, Paris, Cerf, 1970, p. 80; *De Opificio mundi*, 21, ed. R. Arnaldez, Paris, Cerf, 1961, p. 154; citation from Plato (*Timaeus*, 29e).
39 L. Chestov, *Athènes et Jérusalem*, IV, 28, ed. A. Paris, Milan, Bompiani, 2005, p. 1112.

remedy this invisibility by making an image of Him (*Ex.*, 20, 4). This means two things.

(1) On one hand, it is as impossible to know and define man as it is God, the Model of which he is the copy. The Greek Father of the Church, Gregory of Nyssa, who will be followed in this by many others, put it in syllogistic form as early as the fourth century: man is in the image of God; now, God is unknowable; hence man is himself also unknowable.[40] It is impossible to enclose man's freedom in a definition. Man is good in this sense, that he is capable of deciding what he will be.

Günther Anders clearly saw the connection between the enterprise of a philosophical anthropology and that of a theology. In his case, it was to deduce from atheism the impossibility of any anthropology.[41] One can note this. Furthermore, one can be tempted to make use of the point for apologetic aims, to cry "ah, ha!" in triumph, and draw the consequence of the necessity of some theology to establish a discourse (*logos*) concerning man (*ánthrōpos*). In all that there would· be a grain of truth. But it would be precipitous to be satisfied with it. This is because the affirmation of being created in the image of God is precisely what renders any anthropology essentially provisional. The image, in this case man, will be as impossible to define as its divine Model.

(2) On the other hand, it is impossible to take such a God as a model. To be sure, it is a matter of "imitating God," and it was not without reason that the Fathers of the Church incorporated a Platonic formulation into their theory of mysticism.[42] But what kind of God are we to imitate? If we have to imitate a

40 Gregory of Nyssa, *De la création de l'homme*, chap. XI; PG, 44, 156bc; see on this passage and others the commentary of J.-L. Marion, *Certitudes négatives*, Paris, Grasset, 2010, pp. 66–74.
41 G. Anders, "Die Antiquiertheit der philosophischen Anthropologie" [1979], *Antiquiertheit*, t. II, pp. 128–30.
42 Plato, *Theaetetus*, 176b, then H. Merki, ΟΜΟΙΩΣΙΣ ΘΕΩ. *Von der platonischen Angleichung an Gott zur Gottähnlichkeit bei Gregor von Nyssa*, Fribourg, Paulusverlag, 1952.

visible god, we would choose to make his attributes our own, and to the highest degree. We then would deck ourselves out with the thunder of Zeus, the winged sandals of Hermes, or even—allow us a bit of frankness, if you will—the majestic organ of Priapus.

The only way of imitating an invisible God, who does not give Himself in any other image than that which produces his imitation in us, is liberty.

Providence, project, task

Thus, there must be an external point of reference to have the right to say of man that he is worth the trouble of existing. According to the Bible, God constitutes an Archimedean point of this sort. He affirms man. This, of course, does not mean that he gives man a blank check, that he legitimates any and all human caprices. Thus, for example, it is wrong to attribute to the Bible, and more precisely to the creation account of man in *Genesis*, responsibility for the contemporary devastation of the earth. This has been shown by examining the way in which the verses in which the God of *Genesis* enjoins man to be fruitful, to multiply and have dominion over the earth (*Genesis*, 1, 28), have been commented on in the Jewish and Christian exegetical traditions. The accent is never put on dominion or domination, but always on fruitfulness.[43] And where superiority is mentioned, it is supposed to recall an innate nobility, one that is peacefully possessed, not violently acquired. In no way is it intended to encourage an upstart to claim rights he doesn't possess, by crying even more loudly that "he isn't a nobody." As for dominion, most of the time it is interpreted as an allegory for the dominion of the human over the bestial in man himself.

The dialogue with Foucault allowed us to better understand an aspect of this question. In response to the critique of humanism

---

43 See J. Cohen, *"Be Fertile and Increase, Fill the Earth and Master It." The Ancient and Medieval Career of a Biblical Text*, Ithaca and London, Cornell University Press, 1989.

that he offered, I proposed to consider man as *plenipotentiary*, and hence responsible. But I left open the questions: responsible for what exactly? And invested with what mission, exactly?

I can now answer: nothing other than *being*.

Chapter IX
Being as a Command

To clarify the result with which I concluded the previous chapter, I need to take a second look at the first creation account. To this point, I have placed myself inside the text. Now I need to look at it in context. My guiding thread will be the following question: Why did this account figure at the beginning of the Pentateuch? To be sure, as we indicated it is a grand attack on an alternative position, but if it truly is an opening movement, one should discover its themes in what follows.

Commands, people, land

In the whole they form, the five opening books of the Bible, the Pentateuch, have been known under the name of the "Law" (*nomos*) of Moses, ever since the Greek translation of the Septuagint in the third century before Jesus Christ. Now, it can be the case that the term "law" is not perfectly adequate to convey the meaning of Torah; many have made this case. Still, the majority of the five books that open the Bible consist in commands.

One then can ask what to make of the narratives that interrupt the legislative texts, and especially those that come before them and make up the entirety of the first book, *Genesis*. And in fact the "Sages," the rabbis of the Talmud, in particular Rabbi Isaac, asked why the Torah did not begin with the first command, that of having to observe the Passover (*Ex.*, 12, 2), or at least the Decalogue. The classic commentary of Rashi reproduced one of the answers: the history that is recounted legitimates the possession of the holy land by the people of Israel who, if they could not produce this title of ownership, would be easily accused of theft by the nations that were dispossessed, even exterminated.[1] However, it is not simply a matter of an ideological justification of a conquest, even if we do possess traces of an accusation of that sort, which could have elicited such a response.[2] In fact, the occupied land is not just the site of agricultural exploitation or the domain for the exercise of a political authority. Above all it is the place where the Law can be fulfilled in its fullness, unlike the various lands of exile where its application can only be partial. The Law requires the land, it is the law of a land.

My own answer will be similar. The creation narrative is not foreign to the theme of "command." In fact, it constitutes the first appearance of commands, and provides the key for all the others. The sacred history that is recounted in the Pentateuch is structured by the giving of commands. This history is the history of a law that seeks a people that it can claim. During the course of this history, several volleys of commands are launched, each having its own specific recipient and executor. Finally, the decisive salvo encounters a ready people. The history, designated in Hebrew by a word that originally meant "generations" (*toledoth*), is that of the genealogy of a people who would be able to receive the Law. This idea remained quite vivid in Jewish consciousness, and is found in the gravity of the Talmud as well as a host of jocular presentations of God as the one who sought a people to whom he could palm off the somewhat embarrassing morality that he just formulated.

The rhythm of the commands

The Pentateuch presents us with a great number of negative and positive commands, of orders and interdictions. They are distributed in successive groups. I distinguish five. Let us survey them in the reverse order of their appearance.

1   See my work *The Law of God: The Philosophical History of An Idea.* Translated by Lydia G. Cochrane (Chicago: The University of Chicago Press, 2007).
2   See, for example, Procope, *Vandalenkriege*, II, 10 [= IV, 10], # 12–22, ed. O. Veh, Munich, Heimeran, 1971, pp. 230–32; also cited by N. Machiavel, *Discorsi*, II, 8, in *Tutte le opere, op. cit.*, t. I, p. 253.

(1) The Torah of Moses in its entirety, according to the count established by the Sages of the Talmud, contains six hundred and thirteen commandments. They are distributed in the four last books of the Pentateuch, which contains injunctions and interdictions starting from—we just recalled this—*Exodus* 12, 2. According to certain of these same sages the number indicates a totalizing intention: three hundred and sixty-five prohibitions, one for each day, and two hundred and eighty-eight positive commandments, one for each organ of the human body.[3]

The positive and negative commands are addressed to an Israel established on a land that it cultivates, living under the authority of a king, offering sacrifices at the Temple. They constitute the charter of the people of Israel.

They subsequently form that of the dispersed Jewish people, deprived of the other markers of its identity: the land, language, king, Temple. They allow it to distinguish itself from the other peoples, "the nations."[4] They establish, as it were, a wall around it, which, even before the destruction of the Temple, came to replace the lost political borders.[5]

(2) The Decalogue was given to a people barely liberated from servitude in Egypt. The ten words that it contains are addressed to free men and lay out the implications of this liberty: "What prevents being free, this is what is forbidden."[6] The God of Israel presents himself as the liberator (*Ex.* 20, 2). And He forbids that anyone would take as his supreme reference anyone (or anything) other than the liberator himself (*ibid.*, v. 3). The liberty thus acquired requires reciprocity: it is forbidden that the God who

3   *bMakkot*, 23b.
4   See Flavius Josephus, *Antiquités judaïques*, I, X, 5, # 192, ed. B. Niese, Berlin, Weidmann, 1955 [= 1887], p. 47 [on circumcision]; Maimonides, *Guide des égarés*, III, 49, *op. cit.*, p. 418. Negatively, this is the source of the repeated reproach of *amixia*: see Tacitus, *Historiae*, V, v, 2.
5   *Lettre d'Aristée à Philocrate*, # 139, *op. cit.*, p. 170; Flavius Josephus, *Guerre des Juifs*, II, 18, 7, # 488, ed. G. Vitucci, Milan, Mondadori, 1974, p. 418.

liberates is deprived of his freedom by being enclosed in an image (vv. 4–6) or in a formula (v. 7). And He asks that this liberty be extended by granting it in turn to whomever (or whatever) depends upon the free men: servants, even domestic animals (vv. 8–11). He requires respect for the parents who assure our legitimacy and made us free children (v. 12).[7] He forbids anyone to treat his neighbor like an animal that one can sacrifice (v. 13) or an object that one can steal (vv. 14–15).

(3) Before that there is a group of seven commands that are not cited in the Bible. The Bible limits itself to alluding to them in a passage where God gives Noah, just emerged from the ark, authorization to eat meat, but on the condition of not eating the blood (*Genesis*, 9. 4). It is only the Talmud that provides a list of the seven commands that address the totality of humanity, and not just the people of Israel.[8]

Given their content, and its relevance to my present argument, I need to devote special attention to them. As I said, they are taken to concern the human race as such and the totality of individuals who make it up.

Among these seven commands, six, which were already revealed to Adam, were merely reiterated to Noah; the seventh, which forbids eating a member of a living animal (*eyvar min hay*), would have been added, because Adam only had the right to a vegetarian diet.[9] More than a simple forbidding of

---

6   See P. Beauchamp, *D'une montagne à l'autre. La Loi de Dieu*, Paris, Seuil, 1999, p. 33.

7   See the Hebrew *ben horin* or the Latin *liber*, on which E. Benveniste, *Vocabulaire des institutions indo-européennes*, Paris, Minuit, 1969, t. I, pp. 321–22.

8   See b*Sanhédrin*, 561; Maimonides, *Mishneh Torah*, "Sanhédrin," IX, 1; H. Cohen, *Religion der Vernunft aus den Quellen des Judentums* [1919], Cologne, Melzer, 1949, pp. 135–48 and 381–88.

9   See *Midrash Bereshit Rabba*, XVI, 6, ed. J. Theodor and Ch. Albeck [Hebrew], Jerusalem, Wahrmann, 1965 (2nd ed.), t. I, pp. 149–51; and M. Mendelssohn, "Schreiben an Herrn Diaconus Lavater" [1769], in *Gesammelte Schriften*, Stuttgart, Frommann Holzboog, t. VII, 1974, p. 11, n. b.

the life of the hunter,[10] this is a matter of a fundamental human trait.

All these commands thus define the basic conditions of the human and in that way sketch an anthropology. They especially include the two characteristics that Claude Levi-Strauss identified as constitutive of the human, to wit: the prohibition of incest and the preparation of food (cooking).[11] The human is thereby distinguished from the animal who copulates with the first partner who comes by, without any concern for the eventual lines of kinship, and which eats its prey raw.

One can interpret in the same way the command to establish tribunals. It distinguishes man from male animals who dispute over a female. It even distinguishes him from the two protohuman adversaries Hegel puts on stage in the prehistory he imagines, whose struggle will decide who will be master and who slave. Fully humanized man knows justice. Its appearance in human relations is concretized by the introduction between two adversaries of a third party who is to judge between them in an impartial manner.[12]

The giver of these commands is named *Elohim* (*Genesis*, 9, 1.6.8). To be sure, this means "God." But a god who appears under a certain angle. Not as the "historical" God, whose name, YHWH, is understood as guaranteeing that He "will be what He will be" throughout the entire adventure He begins with his people (*Ex.*, 3,14), but rather as a "natural" god, the final reference and guarantor of the basic rules of decency. It is the fear of this god that Abraham worried he would not find among the Amalekites, who then would not have respected his marriage (*Genesis*, 20, 11). Or again: it is this god that the "foolish" (*Ps.* 14, 1) does not acknowledge in his "heart" (which is roughly equivalent to his conscience). In fact, he is the "egoist" (*naval*), who only considers his own self-interest and ignores the laws of hospitality,

10 E. Kant, *Zum ewigen Frieden*, 1ˢᵗ Addition, in *Werke*, *op. cit.*, t. VI, p. 221.
11 C. Lévi-Strauss, *Les Structures élémentaires de la parenté*, Paris, PUF, 1949; *Mythologiques*, t. I: *Le Cru et le Cuit*, Paris, Plon, 1964.
12 See G. W. F. Hegel, *Phänomenologie des Geistes*, ed. J. Hoffmeister, Hamburg, Meiner, 1937, pp. 141–50, then A. Kojève, *Esquisse d'une phénoménologie du droit. Exposé provisoire*, Paris, Gallimard, 1981, # 7, p. 24; # 14, pp. 73–75.

refusing to owe anything to anyone else. The "wisdom" whose absence makes him "foolish" is the Egyptian *ma'at*, understood as the fundamental requirement of reciprocity among humans.[13]

I will not include in the list of successive volleys of commands the imperatives found in *Genesis* between the first creation account and the leaving of the ark or, even further, the history of the Patriarchs. These are orders addressed to particular individuals like Abraham or Moses, not commands of universal import.

In the second creation account (*Genesis*, 2, 4b-3, 24), "Adam" designates Man in general more than a particular person. I however understand the injunction addressed to him not to eat of the fruit of the tree of the knowledge of good and evil (*Genesis*, 2, 17) not as a prohibition followed by the threat of a sanction, but rather as a warning putting man on guard against the consequences of a dangerous action.

(4) In the text at the very beginning of *Genesis* that I am commenting on here, there are two groups of declarations. The command to reproduce is given two times. God blesses the animals and says, uttering a monologue before the mute animals: "Be fruitful and multiply" (*Genesis*, 1, 22). Then he blesses the first human couple and utters a command of the same tenor, but which this time is addressed to a recipient (*lahem*) capable of understanding (*ibid.*, v. 28). This is a matter of respecting the inner logic of every living being whose species only subsists by gliding, or as it were by surfing, on the individuals who are born and die.

The divine benediction is not a way of adding the sacred to what would otherwise remain profane and simply biological. It is that by which God stirs the fecundity latent in each creature.

At the same time, the slight addition without which the two sentences would be strictly parallel subtly indicates the chasm that separates the things about which one speaks and the persons one addresses.

(5) The very first command is only a quasi-command. It is expressed by a simple imperative, that of the verb "to be," itself the simplest of all: "Be!" Technically speaking, this is what Hebrew grammar calls a "jussive." The imperative in the strict sense is

13 See J. Assmann, *Ma'at. Gerechtigkeit und Unsterblichkeit im alten Ägypten*, Munich, Beck, 1995, pp. 58–91.

excluded here because to this point there is nothing or no one who could obey the order. The jussive of the verb "to be" (*hayah*) is not found elsewhere in the Bible except with a complement introduced by a preposition: "Let her be for you <as a spouse>" (*Judges*, 15, 2); Let not your hand be on him" (I *Samuel*, 18, 17). The creation account is the only known passage where it is employed absolutely, and this exception is called for by the thing itself.

What is to be at once the content and the recipient (yet-to-come) of this first command is nothing else but light. It is to it that it is commanded to be, as well as the objects that emit it: the celestial vault as lampstand (v. 6) and the two "lamps" that hang from it (v. 14). How should one make sense of this affinity between light and the "Be!"? Perhaps one should see here a prephilosophical way of viewing an analogy between light and Being that philosophy will later articulate. The light that allows us to see is itself invisible; it only allows itself to be seen indirectly, on the surfaces it illumines, whose colors its displays. In the same way, Being refuses to be directly grasped and only reveals itself in the beings it causes to be.

One can summarize all this in the tables that follow.

Number	(1)	1 (2x.)
Reference	*Genesis*, 1, 3.6.14	*Genesis*, 1, 22.28
Statement	Without partner	Soliloquy (1, 22) then order (1, 28)
Recipient	All that is (light, firmament, lights)	The living, sea animals and birds; man, male and female
Injunction	Be! ("Let it be!")	Increase and multiply! = Be alive as a species!
Contrary	Nothing	Inanimate
Realization	Existence	Life

7	10	61
Genesis, 9, 9–17 bSanhedrin, 56a	*Exodus*, 20, 2–17	All the Torah after *Exodus*, 12, 2
Dictated by God (*elohim*)	Dictated by God who presents himself as YHWH (v. 2)	By the intermediary of Moses
Every man issued from Noah: every man	Israel having left Egypt: the free man	Israel installed in its land, under its king, around its Temple
Be a man!	Be a free man!	Be an Israelite/Jew!
Animal	Slave	Nations
* Relation open to Transcendence (no idolatry) * Prohibition of incest (*giluy 'erayot*) * Diet (*eyvar min hay*) * Language (no blasphemy) * Respect for life (no murder) * Respect for freedom (no kidnapping) * Tribunals: a third party between two adversaries	* No other god but the liberator * No image * No invoking the Name * slave = Sabbath rest * parents = respect *the other = don't kill * wife = fidelity * goods = don't steal * truth = no false witness * neighbor = no envy	Rules for all of life 365 prohibitions for the entire year 248 orders for all the organs of the human body bMakkot, 23b

An ethics of distinction

Each series of commands places a reality before, and against, its contrary. It is a matter of detaching oneself from what one is not: from the nations of the world, from slaves and servile human beings (whatever their social status), from animals, from inanimate minerals, finally from nothing, pure and simple.

The first creation account is marked by an essential theme, that of separation: God separates light from darkness, the firmament separates the waters above from those below.[14]

The underlying morality is thus a morality of *distinction*, with this term being taken in its social sense, but also in its most general sense. The Bible begins by distinguishing being from nothing. To paraphrase St. Bonaventure a bit freely: "Being does not arrive in person and unadulterated except in the full rout of non-being" (*ipsum esse purissimum non occurrit nisi in plena fuga non esse*).[15]

From this one can draw an important consequence concerning the sanctions attached to the failure to obey the commands. Most deeply, this is nothing other than leaving the domain of what one really is, the loss of the characteristics that define one, and entrance into a specific form of non-being: ceasing to be a Jew and becoming *goy*, ceasing to be a free man and becoming a slave, ceasing to be a human being and becoming an animal, ceasing to be a living thing and dying, ceasing to be an existent and disappearing.

In this way, each group of commands has the function of defining the group that receives it. To be a Jew is to obey the Torah. In the same way, to be a free man living in society is to respect the ten commandments; to be a man, is to live according to the seven commands given to Noah; and so on.

Thus, all of biblical "morality" is aristocratic. One could entertain oneself profitably by reading various aspects of the

14 See P. Beauchamp, *Création et séparation. Étude exégétique du chapitre premier de la Genèse*, Paris, Desclée de Brouwer, 1969, pp. 50, 58, 294 and 372.
15 St. Bonaventure, *Itinerarium mentis ad Deum*, V, 3, in *Opera Omnia*, Ex Typographia Collegii S. Bonaventurae, t. 5 (1891), p. 308b.

Decalogue in an aristocratic key, as the portrait of the ideal gentleman: a well-born man will not bow before a sculpted or painted image (*Ex.*, 20, 5); he will not tell fibs (v. 7, 16); he grants his manservant a day of rest (vv. 8-10); he has a lively awareness of the respect due to his lineage, and regularly visits the gallery of his ancestors in his home (v. 12); he doesn't involve himself in dirty business such as killing, or deceiving his wife, or robbing a store (vv. 13, 15); he doesn't lower himself to desire the possessions of others (v. 17).

It happens that this "aristocratic" dimension has been recognized. Hence the formulation of Rabbi Yehoshua ben Levi, which perhaps was directed against a certain understanding of St. Paul: he is not a free man, that is, a noble man, well-born (*ben hōrin*), except he who obeys the Torah.[16]

This morality, however, is not cast in the form of the imperative, as Kant's, nor in the optative,[17] as Victor Brochard nicely put it in connection with Greek morality, but rather, quite simply, in the indicative. There are equivalents in ordinary life of this biblical morality: "A gentleman does not cheat at cards." Not: A gentlemen *ought not* to cheat . . . This is a description. To disobey a rule, what is called "sinning," is at bottom *derogation*, by that very fact losing the quality to which one was called or could claim. This is what makes the formula tautological: a gentleman is recognized by the fact that he refuses to do this or that; the one who would lower himself to do it would thus reveal someone who is not what he imagined himself to be.

In such an ethic, the imperative, if it appears, is at the service of the indicative. It aims at nothing more than a simple recall to order, in all the senses of the latter term.

16 *Pirqey Aboth*, VI, 2. Other examples in E. E. Urbach, *The Sages. Their Concepts and Beliefs* [trans. I. Abrahams], Jerusalem, Magnes Press, 1979, pp. 258, 295, 302, 427 ff.

17 V. Brochard, "La morale ancienne et la morale moderne" [1901], *Études de philosophie ancienne et de philosophie moderne*, Paris, Alcan, 1912, p. 492.

Refractions of the "Be!"

The first command, as we said, is not yet truly a command, because it does not address itself to someone or something that could hear and obey it. The "Be!" is rather a "Let it be!"

Nonetheless, this quasi-command confers their form on the contents of those that follow. To be what one is, behold the content of the command that engenders all the others: "Be what you are!", to wit (according to the case): (a) a being; (b) a living thing; (c) a man; (d) a free man; (e) a Jew. Respect what constitutes you as what or who you are! There is therefore no "obedience" to any thing other than the principle of what one is.

Let us look closer at the first (quasi-)command: "Be!" An abyss separates it from the second: "Be fruitful and multiply." This chasm, to speak the language of traditional metaphysics, is nothing other than the ontological difference between *existentia* and *essentia*. The second commandment bears upon what is already endowed with an essence and which, for example, is a sea animal or a bird, a human male or female.

In an earlier work, I attempted to identify what seems to me a fundamental characteristic of the biblical God. To sum up in a formulation that I believe I have demonstrated: God doesn't *ask* anything of us, but he *expects* us to produce the spontaneous, "natural," effects of what we are. Thus, since we are rational and social beings, he expects justice from us, which is the work of reason and the condition of life in society. He thus expects nothing more from us than to be what we are.[18] I was able to establish this point only on the plane of human action. Here I can develop and generalize it to the entirety of the created.

The commands fundamentally reduce to a single one, of which they are the various imprints, or if one prefers another image, *refractions* which vary according to the medium through which they pass. The first command, that of creation, opens a series of

---

18 See my work *On the God of the Christians (and on one or two others)*, trans. Paul Seaton (St. Bend, IN: St. Augustine Press, 2013).

commands that refract the first while passing through different prisms. I borrow refraction as a luminous image from *Genesis* 1, although by way of an anachronism since the author of *Genesis* 1 did not have the slightest idea of Newton's optics, and for good reason. Light was created in the very first place. In it God can "see" that what he created is good. The being that is thus enjoined is refracted and broken down, as it were, into the living, the human, the free human, and the Jew.

This unique and fundamental command is the first of all the "orders" that the Creator gives according to the *Genesis* account: "Be!" (*yeh*). Being is a commandment.

This command is pregnant with all the meanings of "being": in technical Latin terms, it contains *existentia* (to be present, to exist) as well as *essentia* (to be what one is). More simply, it implies not only that it is good to exist, but that it is good for each being to coincide with what it is.

In particular, man is obliged to be human. Obliged by what engagement? By nothing other than the logic of his own being. How to be human, how to distinguish oneself from the prehuman, how to guard oneself from the inhuman? This is what all the formulas specify, which are somewhat maladroitly called "commandments."

The creative Word

In other texts, the Bible meditated on the creative command. Thus, the Psalms twice repeat the "He spoke" and <it> was, He commanded and <that> stood forth" (*ki hu amar way-yehi, hu siwwa wa-ya'amod*) (*Ps.* 33, 9) and "He commanded and they were created" (*ki hu siwwa we-nivre'u*) (*Ps.* 148, 5).

Presentations like this of a creative word are elsewhere attested to in the ancient Middle East, even before the biblical writings. The word of certain gods, obviously each time the most powerful in a certain pantheon, is deemed to realize itself automatically.[19]

19 See the texts gathered in O. Grether, *Name und Wort Gottes im Alten Testament*, Giessen, Töpelmann, 1934, pp. 139–44.

The thinkers of Islam had to reflect upon a similar formulation, which is found at several places in the Koran. God there says "Be!" and "<the thing> is" (*kun fa-yak nu*).[20] Some deduced that the imperative was the first of all the modes. This was the case, for example, with the Ismailian propagandist Nasir-i Khusraw.[21]

The first divine word, "let the light be," provided the key example of sublime speech for the pseudo-Longinus, the author of the ancient treatise which made the term "sublime" a central concept in the theory of art.[22] And in his oratorio *The Creation* (1798), Joseph Haydn give the appearance of light a musical illustration worthy of genius.

It is well known that Christian theology interpreted the creative word of the God of *Genesis* as the prefiguration of the person (hypostasis) of the Word in the Trinity. The opening words of the *Gospel according to St. John* announce this interpretation by opening with the very same words, *en arkhē*, which open the Greek translation of the first creation account—an obviously self-conscious repetition of *Genesis*. In a magnificent poetic manner, Milton placed the idea in an interior dialogue that God has with Himself, between the Father and the Word: *And thou my Word, begotten Son, by thee/This I perform; speak thou, and be it done. [. . .] So spake the Almighty, and to which he spake/His word, the Filial Godhead, gave effect.*[23]

If this is the case, one understands better a characteristic of Jesus of Nazareth, in whom Christians confess "the Word made flesh" (*St. John*, 1, 14). He adds no new commandment to the orders and prohibitions already present in the Law of Moses. He contents himself with giving them a new basis in his passion and resurrection.[24] Now one understands the reason for this new

---

20 *Koran*, 36, 82; see also 2, 117; 3, 59—apropos to the creation of Jesus.
21 See S. M. Stern, "The Earliest Cosmological Doctrines of Ismailism," *Studies in Early Ismailism*, Jerusalem, Magnes Press, 1983, pp. 3–29.
22 Longinus, *Du sublime*, IX, 9, ed. and trans. H. Lebègue, Paris, Les Belles Lettres, 1939, p. 14.
23 Milton, *Paradise Lost*, VII, 163–64, 173–75.
24 See my work *The Law of God, op. cit.*

attitude: it is nothing other than the fact that the creative command that Jesus "incarnates" already recapitulates the totality of the injunctions that the Law distributes throughout the Pentateuch.

To be, however . . .

Then, why commands? Can't one simply let things happen and simply be what they are? Especially since in any event, and by definition, they already are what they are? Why add ought-to be to to-be? This, for example, is what Machiavelli did. His entire corpus orders us to do what, according to him, we already do, and what everyone has done since the world became a world, and will do as long as there are men.[25] But here, precisely in contrast to what happens in Machiavelli, it is not being that is complicated by a basically superfluous ought-to be. Rather, it is being that emanates from an original ought-to be.

The German writer Erich Kästner, the author of the world-renowned *Emil and the Detectives*, penned a verse that in his country has almost become a proverb: "There is no other good than that which one does." (*Es gibt nichts gutes/außer: Man tut es*).[26] A fine and noble formulation. But it admits a sizeable exception. What to do, in truth, with the good that (perhaps) constitutes our own existence? This is a good that we cannot make, because we are not yet there to make it, but which makes us, so to speak.

Being must become the object of a command, because being is not what we want [*voulons*] and must be enjoined upon us. We certainly want [*voulons*] to continue to live, because to continue to do something is a form of inertia, that is to say, of death. Nietzsche partially grasped this in his critique of the idea of "the will to live," which he had found in Schopenhauer and which he rejected in favor of his "will to power." The desire of a life that is already ours

25 See P. Manent, *Naissances de la politique moderne*, Paris, Payot, 1977, p. 10.
26 E. Kästner, "Moral", *Zeitgenossen, haufenweise. Gedichte*, ed. Harald Hartung, Munich, Hanser, 1998, p. 277 [= Werke, B. 1].

(see Heidegger's *Jemeinigkeit*) is in fact a desire for death—not to experience dying, but to be dead. Freud saw this when he introduced the death-wish.[27]

Leibniz speaks of a tendency of possibilities to realize themselves by passing into existence (*conatus ad existentiam*), and Nietzsche reprised the idea by having his Zarathustra say: "All the brave things volunteer and plunge joyfully into existence" (*Alle guten mutwilligen Dinge springen vor Lust ins Dasein*).[28]

Fine formulations too. But do we have the means to realize them, if there is no one to call into being? Only the divine command legitimates being by declaring it "good." This implies that God is beyond Being, like Plato's Good.[29]

Primacy of logos

From the point of view of the history of ideas, it is well known that the prologue of *St. John's Gospel*, "In the beginning was the Word," came from the exegesis of *Genesis* 1:1. Enormous energy has been devoted to meditating upon the meaning of this Word, and profound interpretations have been proposed. In particular, it has been made clear that to make creation a work of the Word implies the affirmation of the rationality of the universe, and hence to make it in principle intelligible and accessible to human reason. This seems perfectly reasonable to me. However, there is another dimension of *logos* that I would like to highlight here, a dimension that seems to me faithful to the primacy of practical reason discovered by Kant. According to the German philosopher, reason (*Vernunft*) is not truly itself except when it is practical.[30]

27 S. Freud, *Jenseits des Lustprinzips* [1920], chap. V–VI.
28 G. W. Leibniz, "Vingt-quatre thèses sur la métaphysique," # 5, in *Oeuvres et fragments inédits*, ed. L. Couturat, Hildesheim, Olms, 1966 [= 1903], p. 534; F. Nietzsche, *Also Sprach Zarathustra*, III, "Auf dem Ölberge," in KSA, t. IV, p. 219.
29 Plato, *Republic*, VI, 509b.
30 E. Kant, "Primat der praktischen Vernunft," *Kritik der praktischen Vernunft, op. cit.*, pp. 138–40.

In the biblical text, *logos* exists first of all as command. The first command, that of creation, is just as practical as those that follow it, it is even the purest form of morality. *Logos* exists first of all as creative liberty, the other forms of it are derivative.

"Be what you are" thus appears as the first commandment. With this specification, that the relationship between ought-to be and to be is reversed: one does not find the claim to derive the ought from the is which was critiqued by Hume, and which has been called "the naturalistic fallacy" ever since G. E. Moore.[31] On the contrary, the first command is purely moral, and even the purest form of morality, to wit: "Be what you ought to be!" Not: "Follow your nature!", according to the Stoic formulation (*homologoumenōs tè physei zèn*), but rather: "Follow what called your nature into being!"

The Good can be defined as what is as it ought to be, as the conformity of Being (*is/Sein*) to Ought-to be (*ought/Sollen*). Now, this is precisely the case of what is created, to the extent it flows from the command "Be!" Since God is limited by nothing, what He makes cannot but be good. What is created is therefore necessarily good. In this way, the observation that "He saw that it was good" becomes a kind of tautology.

To act in order to be

Ever since Plato a problem has preoccupied philosophical reflection on religion. In the *Euthyphro*, Plato has Socrates ask if what is holy (*to hosion*) is so because it pleases the gods or, rather, if it pleases the gods because it's so.[32] The problem was restated in a modified form in Judaism, Christianity, and Islam: Is the good, good, because God commands it, or does God command it because it is good? The thinkers of Muslim apologetics (Kalām) in its dominant strand, and in Christian lands certain extreme nominalists, answered that God sovereignly and arbitrarily decides what is good and simply

31 G. E. Moore, *Principia Ethica*, I, # 10, *op. cit.*, p. 62 ff.
32 Plato, *Euthyphro*, 10d.

imposes it. Other thinkers, to my mind better advised, answer that the good that God commands is only an aspect of God himself. In that way, there is no need to opt for "values" that would be external to him and to which he would be obliged to submit. This is what the theologians who incline toward the first view want to avoid at all costs, and not without reason. The aforementioned "values" are properties of God himself, and are not anything other than Him. They are God refracted in the prism of our creaturely optic.

This alternative, however, disappears in the case of a creative command. In it, the two coincide. And at bottom, God doesn't command anything other than what He "is": "I am" (*Exodus*, 3, 14). "You will say to Israel: "I AM sent me." This designation has the closest connection with the genre of discourse, commands, that will be placed in the mouth of the One who just presented himself. The name "I am" gives the tonality in which to read all the commands that follow.

In that way, the fulfillment of any of the commands is by that very fact an imitation of God. Not in the sense that human virtue models itself on divine virtue. The gods aren't virtuous, as Aristotle already pointed out, and as Plotinus repeated in his way.[33] One can say the same thing about the God in the singular of the Bible. The imitation of God consists, not in *doing*, but rather in *being*.

This does not lead to any sort of paralyzing quietism, however. For in what concerns *us*, we human beings, we aren't except to the extent we act. One thus recoups the intuition inadequately formulated by Sartre earlier.[34]

It is quite possible that there is a "metaphysics of Exodus," in Gilson's famous phrase.[35] But it is important to note that it is also, and above all, a morality. In saying that, I do not want to deny the

---

33 Aristotle, *Nicomachean Ethics*, X, 8, 1178b8–18; Plotinus, *Enneads*, I, 2 [19], 1.
34 See supra, p. 134–135.
35 É. Gilson, *L'Esprit de la philosophie médiévale*, Paris, Vrin, 1989, p. 50, n. 1.

obvious fact that the content of the book of *Exodus*, in its legislative part, can provide rules of conduct that pertain to "morality." Rather, I mean to emphasize that it is *precisely as a morality* that "the metaphysics of Exodus" merits being called a metaphysics.

Beyond the opposition of autonomy and heteronomy

From this point of view, it is important to take a look at a concept which is often taken to be the hermeneutical key to our understanding of the New Testament: the obedience of faith (*hypakoē tēs pisteōs*). It appears in bold letters in St. Paul (*Romans*, 1, 5; 16, 26). It is even placed at the center of Christianity by certain theologians, especially of the Calvinist obedience. They then encounter an objection of Kantian inspiration, that this subjects human freedom to heteronomy. In which case they either seek to circumvent the reproach or they pride themselves on breaking the corrupt will of the sinner.

In fact, however—we need to repeat it—"Be!" is anterior to "Do!" The true command "Do!", different from the simple demand to obey, vulgarly understood as "to submit," is only the derivative specification of the original command "Be!": respect the conditions of your being, be conformed to what you are.

"Become what you are!" is already found in Pindar. The Greek poet counseled the "tyrant" Hiero: "Become such as I teach you that you are" (*genoi' hoios essi mathōn*), i.e., "Show yourself worthy of the qualities that I reveal to you." As a good classicist, Nietzsche knew the formula and simplified it to "Become what you are" (*werde, was Du bist!*).[36] However, in the case that interests us here, it not only adventitious qualities which have to be acquired, but the very essence of what one is.

One begins to understand something of what the Law is when one recapitulates all the commands cast in terms of "Do!" or "Don't do!" in the single command "Be!" which is pregnant with

---

36 (From memory): Pindar, *Pythian Odes*, II, 72; Nietzsche, *Ecce Homo*, subtitle.

all the others and which allows them to flow from it, depending upon the circumstances.

Once one has adopted this perspective, autonomy and heteronomy cease to be opposites and become complementary. The law ceases to be heteronomous and, to the contrary, becomes the guarantee of true autonomy.

In the same way, the two usual meanings of the word "law," the proper sense which is juridical and political, and the metaphorical sense according to which we speak of "laws of nature," reconnect to the point of coinciding. The positive law reduces to the injunction addressed to each being to observe in absolute fidelity the conditions of its own existence.

The commands that come after the first constitute the conditions for existing of all the beings they bear upon, then those to whom they are addressed. Men are perfectly capable of grasping what allows them to lead a harmonious and peaceful existence. For that they do not need a reference to a divine foundation. It suffices for them to understand, thanks to their reason, that certain ways of "doing" permit them to establish themselves in "being." But at this point one remains at the level of a hypothetical imperative: for man, if he ought to have being, then a certain way of "acting" is required. But who can tell us that he ought to have being? In particular, who can tell us that it is good that we *are*, that our very existence, our possessing the characteristics that make us men, is good? Who other than God?

The Origin of the Texts

The present work essentially reproduces a conference of six talks given at the Catholic University of Louvain (Louvain-la-Neuve) while I occupied the Cardinal Mercier chair in 2011. They were given in May on three occasions: the 8th through the 10th; the 16th and 17th; and the 23rd and the 24th.

The first chapter was delivered as the inaugural lecture under the title that the work now possesses. It had already been given in a shorter form before my colleagues at the Institute of France (of the Academy of moral and political sciences) on the 10th of January. It was an opening movement, in the musical sense of the phrase. A good number of the themes that are subsequently developed are initially announced. Hence, its greater length than the chapters that follow.

Chapters II, III, IV, VI, VII and VIII are based on the six talks that followed the inaugural lecture. However, the last section of Chapter II on Günter Anders was written for the present work.

Chapter V on Alexander Blok was not given at the conference, but was written shortly after.

Chapter VII reproduces the essentials of an article that was already published: "La galaxie Blumenberg," *Le Débat*, n. 83, 1995, pp. 173–86.

Chapter IX, even later, develops the one that preceded it and attempts to provide its foundation.

I would like to thank the professors of the University of Louvain for the honor they bestowed on me by inviting me to occupy this prestigious chair. My gratitude goes especially to M. Jean Leclercq, whose influence was decisive and was the most attentive of hosts.

This book of medium length, like the smaller *Les Ancres dans le ciel* that preceded it in 2011, is a kind of satellite to my much longer work, *Le Règne de l'homme*. It should be read, on one hand, as a way of freeing the much longer work of certain developments that could only be summarized in it, and, on the other, as going further, by affirming more directly and with less circumspection what the larger book put forth more prudently, but also in a more long-winded way.

As a consequence, especially because of the first reason, the reader will notice many repetitions between and among these three books, both in the arguments as in the texts cited. I tried to reduce them to the strictly necessary, but they are inevitable and I ask the reader to forgive them.

Elisabetta Basso (Milan) kindly read Chapter VI on Foucault and saved me many mistakes. Claire Vajou helped improve Chapter V on Blok with her knowledge of the Russian language and culture.

The entirety of the manuscript was read by Irène Fernandez and by Françoise, my wife.

To all, my most sincere thanks.

Index

A

Adorno, Theodor W., 45
Aeschylus, 10
Anders, Günther, 34, 35–36, 37–38, 92, 150
Aquinas, Thomas (saint), 101, 129
Arendt, Hannah, 35, 135
Aristodemus, 148
Aristotle, 6, 16–17, 26
Artaud, Antonin, 83, 103
Augustine, 129, 141
Aulus Gellius, 2, 24
Averroes, 127–128

B

Baader, Franz von, 40
Bacon, Francis, xiv, 8–9, 12, 25, 29, 98, 102, 119
Barth, Karl, 73
Baudelaire, Charles, 81
Benatar, David, 54
Benedict XVI (pope), ix, x
Benn, Gottfried, 142
Benson, Robert Hugh, 75
Berdyaev, Nicolas, 77, 105–106, 131
Bergson, Henri, 138
Bernard, Claude, 28
Birkin, Rupert, 14
Blok, Alexander, 73, 75, 76–77, 78, 79, 80–82, 83, 84, 85–88
Bloy, Leon, 105, 128
Blumenberg, Hans, 46, 112–133

Bodin, Jean, 103
Boethius, 142
Bonaventure (saint), 161
Bourdieu, Pierre, 97
Brague, Rémi, ix, xi, xii, xiii, xiv, xv
Breton, André, 141
Broch, Hermann, 50
Brochard, Victor, 162
Buddha, 54, 58
Burckhardt, Jacob, 3
Butler, Samuel, 31, 34
Butterfield, Herbert, 115
Byron, George Gordon (Lord), 53–54

C

Casanova, Paul, 124
Cato the Elder, xi
Chestov, Leon, 149
Cicero, 24
Comte, Auguste, 10, 18, 21, 28, 139
Conrad, Joseph, 49
Cook, James (captain), 104
Copernicus, Nicolaus, 26, 91
Cousin, Victor, 82
Croce, Benedetto, 72

D

Darwin, Charles, 31, 46, 82, 91, 138
Descartes, René, xiv, 8, 9, 118
Desmoulins, Camille, 18

Dilthey, Wilhelm, 115
Diogenes of Sinope, 43
Döblin, Alfred, 13–14
Donoso Cortes, Juan, 21
Dostoyevsky, Fyodor, 21, 52, 84
Duhem, Pierre, 26
Dyson, G. B., 34

E
Eddington, Arthur S., 26
Empedocles, 56
Epicurus, 141–142

F
Facio, Bartolomeo, 69
Fechner, Gustav Theodor, 140
Feuerbach, Ludwig, 108
Fichte, Johann Gotlieb, 8, 9, 35
Flaubert, Gustave, 13
Foucault, Michel, 46, 89–111, 151
France, Anatole, 19
Freud, Sigmund, 91, 167

G
Galilei, Galileo, 27, 28
Garaudy, Roger, 93
Gauchet, Marcel, 96
Gibbon, Edward, 12
Gide, André, 46
Gilson, Étienne, 169
Goethe, Johann Wolfgang von, 78
Goldman, Lucien, 90
Gorky, Maxim, 84
Görres. Joseph von, 40
Grahame, Kenneth, 17
Gray, John N., 3
Gregory of Nyssa, 128

H
Hagen, Karl Heinrich Wilhelm, 2, 11

Haydn, Joseph, 164
Hegel, Georg Wilhelm Friedrich, 79, 108, 157
Heidegger, Martin, 34, 35, 93
Heine, Heinrich, 73–74, 76
Henry, Michael, 27
Herodotus, 40, 130, 141
Herzen, Alexander, 18
Hobbes, Thomas, xiv, 20
Hölderlin, Friedrich, 103
Holyoake, George Jacob, 11
Honegger, Jacob, 77
Horace, xi
Horkheimer, Max, 45
Horstmann, Ulrich, 53
Housman, A. E., 140
Hume, David, 167
Huxley, Thomas, 11

I
Ibn al-Muqaffa,' 58, 61
Ibn Khaldûn, 126
Innocent III (pope), 40

J
Jaeger, Werner, 2
James, William, 72
Jean Olieu (or Olivi), Pierre de, 51
Jesus Christ, 7, 117, 118, 124, 165, 166
Jonas, Hans, 115
Jünger, Ernst, 10

K
Kant, Immanuel, 19, 50, 94, 98–99, 101, 106, 162, 167
Karamazov, Alyosha (character in The Brothers Karamazov), 36–37
Kästner, Erich, 166
Kepler, Johannes, 26
Koyré, Alexandre, 118–119

L
Lasaulx, Ernst von, 40
Lawrence, D. H., 14
Leibniz, Gottfried Wilhelm, 167
Lessing, Gotthold Ephraim, 40
Levi, Yehoshua ben, 162
Levinas, Emmanuel, 19
Levi-Strauss, Claude, 157
Lewis, C. S., 51
Locke, John, 27
Loisy, Alfred, 125
Lothar of Segni, 40
Lotze, Hermann, 36
Lovelock, James, 20
Lubac, Henri de, 21

M
Machiavelli, Niccolò, 52, 166
Maimonides, 69
Maistre, Joseph de, 21
Malebranche, Nicolas, 98
Mallarmé, Stéphane, 103
Malraux, André, 105
Manetti, Gianozzo, 8, 69, 98
Mann, Thomas, 78
Marcion of Sinope, xii
Maritain, Jacques, 73
Marsh, George Perkins, 13
Marx, Karl, 10, 21, 31, 98, 113, 135
Maslama al-Majriti, 69
Maurras, Charles, 21
Mill, John Stuart, 103
Milton, John, 164
Moore, G. E., 31, 167
More, Thomas, 32

N
Napoleon, 19, 138
Nasir-i Khusraw, 164
Needham, Joseph, 118–119
Newton, Isaac, 26, 164

Nietzsche, Friedrich, 8, 18, 21, 46, 47, 50, 69, 76–77, 80, 83, 87, 102, 105, 107, 108, 109, 123, 139, 140, 141, 166, 167

O
Omar Khayyam, 141
Origen, 118
Ortega y Gasset, José, 79
Overbeck, Franz, 118

P
Pascal, Blaise, 101, 128
Petrarch, 11, 12
Philo of Alexandria, 149
Pindar, 170
Plato, xii, 16, 23, 49, 51, 100, 102, 144, 167
Plotinus, 7, 50, 142, 169
Pope, Alexander, 98
Porphyry, 5, 44, 55, 56
Prodicus, 8, 40
Proudhon, Pierre-Joseph, 11, 98
Ptolemy, 26
Pushkin, Alexander, 84, 87, 88
Pythagoras, 55

R
Ratzinger, Joseph, ix
Renan, Ernest, 69, 103
Robespierre, Maximilien, 11
Rorty, Richard, 38
Rousseau, Jean-Jacques, 10, 46
Roussel, Raymond, 103
Ruger, Arnold, 2, 11, 98
Russell, Bertrand, 27
Rutherford, Ernest, 26

S
Sade, Marquis de, 102, 103
Sartre, Jean-Paul, 93, 134, 137, 169

Scheler, Max, 45, 137
Schelling, Friedrich Wilhelm, 134
Schiller, Friedrich, 78, 79
Schlegel, Friedrich, 79
Schopenhauer, Arthur, 3, 54, 143, 166
Schweitzer, Albert, 117
Socrates, 8, 31, 148, 167
Soloviev, Vladimir, 74, 75, 76
Sophocles, 40
Spaemann, Robert, 29
Spencer, Herbert, 31
Spengler, Oswald, 78
Spinoza, Baruch, 24
Spranger, Eduard, 1
Statius, 40
Strauss, Leo, 85
Strindberg, August, 83–84
Swain, Gladys, 97

T
Teilhard de Chardin, Pierre, 93
Trismegistus, Hermes, 47
Turmeda, Anselm, 69

V
Voegelin, Eric, 115, 116
Voigt, Georg, 3, 11, 12
Voltaire, 12, 108, 141

W
Wagner, Richard, 76, 85
Weininger, Otto, 84
Werner, Martin, 117
Winckelmann, Johann Joachim, 40

X
Xenophanes, 108
Xenophon, 148